LUFTWAFFE BOMBERS
VS
BRITISH AA DEFENCES
Britain 1940–41

Donald Nijboer

OSPREY PUBLISHING
Bloomsbury Publishing Plc
Kemp House, Chawley Park, Cumnor Hill, Oxford, OX2 9PH, UK
29 Earlsfort Terrace, Dublin 2, Ireland
1385 Broadway, 5th Floor, New York, NY 10018, USA
E-mail: info@ospreypublishing.com

OSPREY is a trademark of Osprey Publishing Ltd

First published in Great Britain in 2025

A catalogue record for this book is available from the British Library.

ISBN: PB: 9781472865762; eBook 9781472865779; ePDF 9781472865786;
XML 9781472865793

25 26 27 28 29 10 9 8 7 6 5 4 3 2 1

Edited by Tony Holmes
Cover artwork and battlescene by Gareth Hector
Profiles and armament views by Jim Laurier
Map and tactical diagram by www.bounford.com
Index by Fionbar Lyons
Typeset by PDQ Digital Media Solutions, Bungay, UK
Printed by Repro India Ltd

Osprey Publishing supports the Woodland Trust, the UK's leading woodland
conservation charity.

To find out more about our authors and books visit
www.ospreypublishing.com. Here you will find extracts, author interviews,
details of forthcoming events and the option to sign up for our newsletter.

Acknowledgements

The Editor would like to thank Chris Goss and Andy Saunders for the
provision of many of the photographs used in this book. Andy also supplied
key information on some of the actions detailed within the work.

Ju 88 cover artwork

On 12 August 1940, 78 Ju 88As of KG 51 (and possibly KG 54) were
assigned to attack Ventnor radar station and Portsmouth harbour. At the time
Portsmouth was heavily defended by approximately 16 4.5in. and 28 3.7in.
HAA guns, as well as weaponry aboard the veteran French battleship *Courbet*,
which was then moored in the naval dockyard after recently joining the Free
French Naval Forces. Although the bombers targeting Portsmouth did so
unopposed by RAF fighters, the approaching Ju 88s encountered intense and
accurate AA fire. Oberleutnant Eberhard Wildermuth, flying Ju 88A-1 Wk-Nr
4078 9K+BS of KG 51 recalled the attack as follows. 'There was not a cloud
in the sky when at midday we approached Portsmouth across the Isle of
Wight. Over the Isle of Wight, there was a thick layer of smoke caused by Flak
– incredibly, we flew at an altitude of 4,000m right through a witch's cauldron
of exploding shells.' After successfully dropping his bombs, Wildermuth's
Ju 88 was hit by AA fire, sending the Ju 88 into a spin. Wildermuth and his
bombardier managed to bail out and were taken prisoner, but the remaining
two crewmen were killed. Although Portsmouth's naval base was badly
damaged, it came at quite a price for the attackers, with AA batteries claiming
two Ju 88s destroyed and a further seven being credited as shot down by RAF
fighters shortly after they had dropped their bombs. (Artwork by Gareth
Hector)

AA cover artwork

By 30 September 1940, when the Battle of Britain was effectively over, the
Luftwaffe had switched almost exclusively to night raids on London. The early
response to this development from the AA defences was limited, with most
batteries not firing at the incoming raiders. Like the pilots of the RAF's single-
seat fighters sent aloft to engage the bombers, the gunners were essentially
blind at night due to their gun laying equipment not being up to the task of
locating bombers in nocturnal skies. As the raids intensified and political
pressure grew, AA Command was forced to 'do something'. In response,
gunners were ordered to maintain a steady rate of fire during the heaviest
raids. While these blind barrages were a waste of ammunition, they did have
an unforeseen effect. Lt Gen Sir Frederick Pile, Commander-in-Chief of Anti-
Aircraft Command, would subsequently write, 'The volume of fire which
resulted, and which was publicised as a "barrage", was in fact largely wild and
uncontrolled shooting. There were, however, two valuable results from it: the
volume of fire had a deterrent effect upon at least some of the German
aircrews, and there was a marked improvement in civilian morale'. Here, four
3.7in. AA guns from the 1st AA Division unleash a salvo skyward at incoming
Luftwaffe bombers over London in early October 1940. (Artwork by Gareth
Hector)

Previous page

Gunners Stan Lawrence (left) and Ronnie Smith from the 58th (Kent)
HAA Regiment, based south of the Thames Estuary, pose with a propeller
blade from a Ju 88 that has been repurposed as the scoreboard for the 264th
HAA Battery. Only a fraction of the aircraft listed would have probably been
damaged (let alone shot down) by shells fired from the 3.7in. AA guns
assigned to the battery. As with RAF Fighter Command in the summer of
1940, AA Command was prone to rampant overclaiming when it came to
enemy aircraft destroyed during the Battle of Britain. Both Lawrence and
Smith are wearing the 6th AA Division flash on their battledress tunics.
(Andy Saunders Collection)

CONTENTS

INTRODUCTION

The Battle of Britain and following Blitz campaign of 1940–41 must be two of the most chronicled and well-studied aerial battles of World War II. Thousands of books, biographies, thesis papers, documentaries, online narratives, military studies and motion pictures have covered every aspect of the battle, yet new books continue to appear every year. Drilling deep into the archives, historians have been able to show when and where aircraft were shot down, serial numbers of said aircraft and in many cases the pilots responsible.

What is missing in most of these histories is any mention of the important role Anti-Aircraft (AA) Command played in the defence of Britain. It is as if it did not exist. This in large part is due to the extensive coverage of the fighter–versus–fighter and fighter–versus–bomber aspects of the battle. The young brave fighter pilot cut a far more dashing figure than the lowly army gunner manning a heavy anti-aircraft (HAA) gun in some isolated farmer's field.

The Battle of Britain and, to a lesser extent, the Blitz are deeply etched into the British psyche. Many myths still surround the battles and began with Prime Minister Winston Churchill's famous quote, 'Never in the field of human conflict was so much owed by so many to so few'. That single line has continually promoted the idea that a small band of pilots from RAF Fighter Command bravely fought the battle-hardened Luftwaffe and saved the fate of the entire British Empire.

Other enduring myths frame the battle as a 'David and Goliath' affair in which the RAF was outnumbered by the Luftwaffe, and in the summer of 1940 Britain stood alone against an unstoppable Hitler and his armies. The focus of this book is in no way meant to diminish the significance of the contributions, courage and sacrifice of those 2,332 RAF fighter pilots who fought during that desperate summer of 1940. Very few AA personnel were killed during the battle, while 510 fighter pilots lost their lives.

In terms of aircraft strength, both the RAF and Luftwaffe had roughly the same number of fighters and bombers, with the Luftwaffe having more dive-bombers in the summer of 1940. British aircraft production surpassed Germany's output, and the RAF received its first Canadian-built Hawker Hurricanes when 20 were delivered in July 1940. It was also a battle in which German bombers and fighters encountered the world's first integrated air defence system complete with radar, fighters, barrage balloons, searchlights and AA guns in depth. Britain was not 'alone' and it was not just the 'few' who won the battle.

The nation's AA preparation for the aerial battles of 1940–41 had started near the end of World War I. The first London Blitz by conventional aircraft (rather than Zeppelins) commenced on 25 May 1917 when a small number of German Gotha G.IV bombers opened Operation *Turkenkreuz* (Turk's Cross). This bold strategic air campaign coincided with unrestricted U-boat warfare in the waters surrounding the British Isles, which it was hoped would cause a crisis of morale in the population.

Even before the 'Blitz' began, there was debate as to how best to shoot down an aircraft. Many believed the AA gun, rather than the aircraft, would be the key weapon for the city's air defence. Yet despite London being rapidly ringed with AA batteries and the formation of dedicated fighter squadrons to defend the capital, the Gothas enjoyed sufficient success to clearly show the potential of strategic bombing, and the need for a more robust fighter and AA defence.

In 1921, Italian air theorist Gen Giulio Douhet wrote *Il dominio dell'aria* (*Command of the Air*). He believed that aerial bombing would be the decisive arbiter in future wars, rendering large land armies obsolete. His ideas spread to the US and Britain, and in the latter country military theorist Maj Gen J. F. C. Fuller claimed a 'knock out' blow by enemy bombers would reduce London to rubble. An RAF Air Staff estimate made in the late 1930s suggested the newly formed Luftwaffe could deliver up to 2,600 tons of bombs and 875 tons of gas bombs in 24 hours, resulting in 60,000 killed and 100,000 injured on the first day of any future conflict.

The introduction of the all-metal monoplane Martin B-10 bomber into US Army Air Corps service in November 1934 added fuel to the fire being stoked by the air power theorists. With a top speed of 213mph and capable of lifting 2,000lb of bombs, it was faster than the RAF's fabric-covered Hawker Fury biplane fighter – Britain's premier interceptor at that time.

As fear of the bomber grew, many held the view that disarmament, including a ban on

Gunners from the 303rd Battery of the Royal Artillery's 99th AA Regiment man their 3in. gun at ZS10 at Hayes Common, Bromley, in May 1940. In 1939 AA Command had 270 of these World War I era guns available for action in both the HAA and LAA roles. (Author's Collection)

A stepped up formation of Do 17Zs strikes out for its target. Despite being the least capable of the Luftwaffe's medium bombers in 1940, 27 Do 17s led the 15 September attack on London. They were followed by 52 He 111s and another 62 Do 17s. RAF fighters and AA fire shot down 32 bombers on what would later be celebrated as 'Battle of Britain Day'. 15 September was also the last time Do 17s participated in a massed daylight attack on a British target. (Author's Collection)

bombing, or deterrence were the only ways forward. When the *Führer* announced the existence of the Luftwaffe in March 1935, disarmament was quickly pushed aside. In response the British Air Ministry embarked on six successive expansion schemes for the RAF. In May 1936, Expansion Scheme C pushed the RAF's target strength to 3,800 aircraft. It was designed to produce a deterrent bomber force, with 68 squadrons equipped with heavy, medium or light bombers. Over the next two years, the preference for defence by a strong bomber force stripped funding for AA defences.

As a result, in September 1939, the 'approved scale' of HAA guns was 2,232, but by July 1940 there were only some 1,200 such weapons of all types in service. Light AA (LAA) guns were also in short supply, with just 253 in service compared with the approved total of 1,200, and searchlights numbered 2,700 deployed, when the approved total was 4,128. Finally, there were only 1,460 barrage balloons available, with the approved total being 2,600.

As part of Britain's overall air defence system, AA guns were a vital component. A robust defence required both fighters and AA guns to be effective. They cannot be looked at in isolation. AA guns have far too often been framed as less effective at shooting down aircraft when compared to fighters. This is a false metric.

It must be remembered that the first job of AA guns was to force bombers to fly higher (which fighter aircraft could not do), thus decreasing accuracy. Bombing errors from 15,000ft were twice as great as from 5,000ft. More 'hot metal up' meant less 'cold, accurate steel coming down'. Its second job was to break up incoming formations or cause evasive manoeuvres, duly affecting accuracy. A He 111 or Ju 88 forced out of formation by AA fire proved easy prey for RAF fighters. AA fire also had some real and important less visible effects. It caused a great deal of damage that in turn had a delayed impact. Punctured fuel or hydraulic lines and holed oil tanks forced many bombers to ditch in the English Channel or crash land upon returning to France. Damaged bombers also required repair, reducing serviceability rates. AA fire also had the power to kill and maim, affecting morale among Luftwaffe bomber crews.

Despite its impressive might and prowess, the Luftwaffe's bomber force that swept through Poland, the Low Countries and France was about to embark on a campaign it had never really planned for. Hitler's *Fall Gelb* (Case Yellow) plan to knock both France and Britain out of the war had failed, for the latter remained very much in the fight. On 16 July 1940, Hitler issued his War Directive No. 16 order that preparations be made for a landing operation against England. The planned cross-Channel invasion of Britain was codenamed *Unternehmen Seelöwe* (Operation *Sealion*).

The Luftwaffe's primary mission in the lead up to *Seelöwe* (planned for 20 September) was to mount an offensive campaign to eliminate the RAF and Royal Navy as a threat to any amphibious landing on British shores. It was a tall order, and given the brief time frame to accomplish the task, it was an almost impossible one. Both the Wehrmacht and the Kriegsmarine lacked the ability to launch an amphibious invasion of Britain. The Kriegsmarine had just one heavy cruiser (*Admiral Hipper*), two light cruisers, seven destroyers and 22 U-boats operational to protect any such crossing. In destroyers alone, the Royal Navy had 69 available for action.

Although in robust shape numerically, the Luftwaffe suffered from poor leadership and limited intelligence of the enemy's strength and disposition. Generalfeldmarschall Hermann Göring, Commander-in-Chief of the Luftwaffe, had no experience in leading an air force in wartime, so he left combat operations to his subordinates, but only up to a point. It was his decision to make London the primary target in early September, and this proved to be a grave mistake. As a result, the Blitz offensive that followed turned into the war's first strategic bombing campaign. Its aim was to knock Britain out of the war by air power alone.

For the coming battles, the Luftwaffe would pit its best bombers – the Dornier Do 17, Heinkel He 111 and Junkers Ju 87 and Ju 88, along with its Bf 109 and Bf 110 fighter-bombers, against AA Command's untested ground defences. Luftwaffe bomber crews were well trained, and their aircraft equipped with some of the most advanced night radio navigation systems in the world.

To meet the coming onslaught, AA Command, which was short of guns, equipment and trained personnel, braced for a Luftwaffe attack that deployed a mix of conventional bombers, dive-bombers and low-level fighter-bombers, and involved both day and night bombing. The contribution of AA Command during the Battle of Britain/Blitz has too often been pushed aside as having been so insignificant as to not warrant any real mention. However, without its efforts, the number of Luftwaffe aircraft shot down or damaged and aircrew killed, wounded or captured would have been lower. To 'The Few' we must add the thousands of gunners and searchlight and barrage balloon operators who manned their posts 24 hours a day and helped the Allies gain their first triumph, setting the cornerstone for final victory against Hitler and fascism.

AA damage sustained by the wing of a He 111 from *Geschwaderstab* KG 27 on 21 March 1941 following a raid on HM Dockyard, Devonport, in Plymouth – this site was bombed on consecutive nights. A jagged hole like this would have taken hours to repair, removing the aircraft from service. As the Battle of Britain wore on, serviceability rates fell, meaning there were fewer aircraft available and a reduced tonnage of bombs being dropped per target. (Chris Goss Collection)

CHRONOLOGY

1925

25 January Air Defence of Great Britain (ADGB) is established.

1933

Spring British Army issues a specification calling for a 3.7in. AA gun. Vickers-Armstrongs delivers the first such weapon in January 1938.

1935

1 March The existence of the Luftwaffe is announced.

1936

June He 111B enters Luftwaffe service with I./KG 157.

21 December The prototype Ju 88 V1, powered by two 1,000hp Daimler Benz DB 600A engines, takes flight.

1937

March First of three Do 17Es enters combat as part of the *Legion Condor* during the Spanish Civil War.

October 4.5in. AA gun enters production.

1938

Summer Work begins on 'modernising' old stocks of World War I-era 3in. AA guns.

22 September *Oberkommando der Luftwaffe* (High Command of the Air Force) develops a study examining the feasibility of an aerial bombing campaign against Britain.

1 November RAF Balloon Command is formed to control all British-based barrage balloons. It would eventually consist of five groups controlling 19 centres (each one of the latter being equivalent to a wing of heavier-than-air aircraft).

1939

April Chain Home (CH) network, consisting of 29 Radio Direction Finding stations, becomes operational along England's southern and eastern coastline.

1 April AA Command is formed with the renaming of the AA Corps. It is led by Lt Gen Alan Brooke.

Summer A total of 190 3.7in. AA guns have been delivered to AA Command.

3 September Britain declares war on Germany. The BBC ceases regional broadcasts to prevent their use for navigation by Luftwaffe bombers.

September AA Command has just 622 HAA guns ready to defend Britain.

6 September First aircraft to be shot down by AA Command is, unfortunately, a Bristol Blenheim IF from No. 64 Sqn.

October Lt Gen Frederick Pile is appointed General Officer Commanding-in-Chief of AA Command. Although an army formation, AA Command comes under the operational control of RAF Fighter Command.

14 October First German air raid of the war and first anti-aircraft engagement when vessels in the Firth of Forth are targeted. RAF fighters shoot

	down two Luftwaffe bombers and AA gunners damage one.
Autumn	First Gun Laying (GL) Mk I radar enters service. By the summer of 1940, 300 are operational.
20 December	An aircraft from the Luftwaffe's *Kampfgruppe* (KGr) 100 pathfinder unit flies to London and back to check the security of the *X-Verfahren* radio navigation system (codenamed 'Ruffian' by RAF Intelligence).

1940

June	Some 1,200 HAA guns of all types are in service across Britain. LAA guns number 3,538. CH radar stations are each defended by three static 40mm Bofors LAA guns.
21 June	Aware of the Luftwaffe's *Knickerbein* (Crooked Leg) navigation beam system, an RAF Anson discovers the beams over the Rolls-Royce factory at Derby.
July	No. 80 Wing – the RAF's first electronic countermeasures unit – is established to coordinate radio countermeasures.
July	Due to a lack of fire control instruments, AA Command abandons most two-gun HAA sites in favour of four-gun layouts.
1 July	The Luftwaffe's specialised fighter-bomber unit, *Erprobungsgruppe* (ErprGr) 210, is formed. The unit is equipped with 30 Bf 109E-4Bs and Bf 110C/Ds.
4 July	Ju 87B Stukas from III./StG 51 raid Portland Harbour. The auxiliary anti-aircraft ship HMS *Foylebank* is sunk, killing 176 sailors. One Ju 87 is shot down by AA fire.
11 July	Portland HAA batteries claim three He 111s destroyed during a raid.
31 July	A total of 1,466 barrage balloons is deployed by 52 squadrons protecting major cities, ports and industrial centres.
July	AA Command claims 26 enemy aircraft shot down for the month of July.
1 August	*Oberkommando der Wehrmacht* (High Command of the Armed Forces) issues the *Führer*'s War Directive No. 17, ordering the Luftwaffe to 'overpower the English air force with all the forces at its command' in order to establish the necessary conditions for the final conquest of England.
10 August	The Luftwaffe has 1,105 He 111s, Ju 88s and Do 17s and 305 Ju 87s available for combat. By the end of August German losses total 744 aircraft to all causes.
13 August	The Luftwaffe launches *Adler Tag* (Eagle Day) – an all-out assault to destroy the RAF in the air and on the ground.
18 August	Luftwaffe losses total 67 aircraft. Ten are credited to Lewis-armed LAA gunners.
21 August	AA Command has just 430 40mm Bofors guns and 7,364 Lewis machine guns in service.
24–25 August	He 111s of *Kampfgeschwader* (KG) 1 accidentally bomb London.
30 August	Hitler authorises the bombing of London.
5–6 September	The Luftwaffe's first night raid on London as a specific target.
7 September	First Luftwaffe daylight raid on London. HAA guns manage to fire just 185 rounds at the intruders.
11 September	AA Command implements 'barrage' fire tactics over London.
16–17 September	Minelaying crews from KGr 126 drop the first of 12 parachute mines on London.

17 September	With the Luftwaffe unable to achieve air superiority over the RAF, the *Führer* postpones the air and sea invasion (*Unternehmen Seelöwe*) of England. This signals the defeat of the Luftwaffe's daylight bombing campaign.
30 September	During the month of September, 260,000 HAA shells are fired over London, but fewer than 12 Luftwaffe bombers are downed.
14–15 November	The centre of Coventry is destroyed by Luftwaffe bombers. AA gunners fire 6,789 HAA rounds into the night sky, destroying just one bomber.
8–9 December	Heaviest Luftwaffe night raid on London sees 115 tons of incendiaries dropped on the capital.

This posed photograph shows a 3.7in. gun with a searchlight in close proximity. Operationally, searchlight clusters were normally situated away from the guns. A cluster was made up of two 120cm searchlights and a master 150cm light. (Author's Collection)

1941

Winter	AA Command's 3in. rocket projectile enters service. The Unrotated Projectile (UP) is fired in salvos of 128 to produce a shotgun effect. Inaccurate and employed in limited numbers, just one salvo is launched at a passing aircraft during the Blitz.
January	Luftwaffe introduces the 2,500kg (5,300lb) (Max) bomb for the first time.
January	Search Light Control (SLC) radar, known as 'Elsie', is introduced in limited numbers.
17–18 April	Last major Luftwaffe night attack on Portsmouth. A Starfish decoy fire on Hayling Island fools the incoming bombers, and only two of the 144 aircraft involved actually drop their bombs on Portsmouth.
May	AA Command's order of battle consists of 1,691 HAA guns, compared with the pre-war approved number of 2,232 for adequate defence.
10–11 May	Final Luftwaffe raid on London is made, *Luftflotten* 2 and 3 generating a total of 571 sorties that inflict severe damage on the city. By the end of the month, the whole of *Luftflotte* (Air Fleet) 2 has been moved east in preparation for Operation *Barbarossa* – the invasion of the Soviet Union.

DESIGN AND DEVELOPMENT

AA COMMAND DEFENCES

In June 1940 Britain possessed the most sophisticated and effective air defence network in the world. While AA Command was desperately short of weapons, RAF Fighter Command was better prepared, with 71 fighter squadrons available. At the outbreak of war AA Command was an army formation, but it came under the operational control of RAF Fighter Command.

Born from the memory of the indiscriminate night bombing by German Zeppelins and Gotha G.IV bombers during World War I, ADGB was established in 1925. It laid down the foundation of what was to become the 'Dowding System' (named after Air Chief Marshal Sir Hugh Dowding, head of RAF Fighter Command), the first integrated fighter defence in operational service in World War II. While the new ADGB initially lacked radar, the principles of the system were the same. The first was the identification of incoming raiders by ground-based observers. Second, personnel manning Observer Corps posts, connected by direct telephone, relayed their information to a reporting centre, which then passed it along to ADGB HQ. There, the third and final act came into play with the timely scramble of intercepting fighters and alert messages sent to all AA gun sites involved, along with searchlight (if it was a night raid) and barrage balloon units.

The limitations of the system were obvious. It only worked in daylight with clear skies, and any approaching bombers had to virtually make landfall before the Observer

A typical CH radar station (this is the installation at Poling, in West Sussex) consisted of three or four 350ft masts supporting the transmitter aerial wires strung horizontally between them. To the right are the all-important receiver, direction-finding and elevation-measuring aerials that were strung from four 240ft tall wooden towers placed in rhombic formation around a blast-proof transmitter building. (Author's Collection)

OPPOSITE BOTTOM

The 3.7in. mobile gun was one of the British Army's most important HAA weapons during the Battle of Britain/Blitz. The mobile version, as seen here, weighed eight tons and had a travel speed along paved roads of just 25mph. Once in place, it could be ready to go into action in 15 minutes. With far too few 3.7in. guns available to it in 1940–41, AA Command was hard-pressed to meet Luftwaffe changes in tactics and target selection. (Chris Goss Collection)

Corps could begin to identify and track enemy aircraft. While fighters and AA guns provided the ADGB with its 'bark' and 'bite', it required 'eyes', a 'brain' and a 'nervous system' to carry information at speed between the latter three to ensure effective opposition to incoming raiders.

By the outbreak of war Britain was well equipped with its CH High and Low radar stations that provided RAF Fighter Command and AA Command with its long-range 'eyes'. Capable of detecting and tracking enemy aircraft approaching at low, medium and high altitudes, CH had a range of more than 100 miles. Once detected, the course, strength and altitude of an incoming raid was sent to the Group and Sector Operations Rooms responsible for their geographic area and, finally, to RAF Fighter Command headquarters at Bentley Priory, near Stanmore in Middlesex. These were the 'brains' of the system, and were linked by landlines – the 'nervous system' – to every squadron and AA, searchlight and barrage balloon battery.

Due to several technological limitations, CH radars could not track targets once they made landfall. Behind the radars was the Observer Corps, which numbered 30,000 personnel. Manning 1,000 observer posts, their job was to report numbers, type of aircraft, position, heading and height directly to their Group and Sector Operations Rooms. The Observer Corps was also backed up by AA gun batteries, whose personnel reported directly to their Operations Rooms when they sighted enemy aircraft. It was a system that worked well, and provided AA ground defences with ample warning of an incoming raid, especially low-level incursions.

Both HAA and LAA guns were used for the point defence of airfields, cities, harbours, radar stations and military factories. In July 1940, AA Command deployed 359 4.5in. (static), 634 3.7in. (mobile and static) and 143 3in. HAA guns for high-altitude defence. For low-level defence, AA Command deployed 3,677 LAA guns in seven types – 366 40mm Bofors guns, 114 'two pounders', 132 3in. guns prepared for LAA work, 37 Hispano-Suiza Mk 1 20mm cannon and no fewer than 3,028 0.303in. Lewis machine guns.

The most numerous type of HAA deployed in Britain was the Vickers-Armstrongs QF (Quick Firing) 3.7in. gun, one of the finest HAA weapons of the war. During the 1920s, the British Army designed several experimental AA guns, and in 1933 issued a specification calling for a 3.7in. gun that could fire a 28lb warhead. Capable of expending ten rounds per minute, it had an effective ceiling of 25,000ft. The exploding shell had a lethal radius of about 45ft.

The newer and heavier Vickers-Armstrongs QF 4.5in. gun was deployed in smaller numbers. To defend its ports, the Admiralty pressed for a weapon specifically designed for the role. The obvious candidate was the existing 4.5in. shipboard gun. The economics in ammunition supply made sense and the War Office accepted the Admiralty's idea, leading to the purchase of the 4.5in. gun. It fired a 55lb shell to an effective ceiling of 26,000ft. The lethal radius of the exploding round was about 60ft.

Backing up these guns, and to fill the many gaps in the 'approved scale' of 2,232 HAA guns required for the minimum defence of Great Britain, was the World War I era QF 3in. 20cwt gun. Its performance was severely limited by a shortage of predictors and height finders. Effective ceiling was 14,000ft. The 3in. guns prepared for the LAA role used deflection sights and were mostly provided with shrapnel shells to engage low-level raiders.

HAA guns were usually deployed in half batteries of four. Depending on the importance of a target, sites with two, six or even eight guns were not uncommon. Each four-gun battery was equipped with its own height-finder and predictor. Once an enemy formation was spotted, the Stroud No. 1 Mk IV height-finder would begin tracking the aircraft. Information from the height-finder was fed directly into the Vickers-Armstrongs Predictor No. 1 Mk III, which calculated the necessary firing solution – the azimuth (bearing) and elevation (height) settings for the guns and the time fusing for the shell. When the firing solution was complete, the predictor sent it via a Mag-slip electrical induction system to dials on each gun in the battery. There, the gunners laid the gun, set the fuze, loaded the shell and fired. Shells for both the 3.7in. and 4.5in. guns used the No. 206 mechanical time fuze, which had a maximum running time of 43 seconds.

Of course, incoming bombers could disrupt the gunner's aim by slight turns, slowing down or climbing as they approached their bomb release. This worked in the gunner's favour, however, for 'jinking' during the final run to the target only decreased accuracy and made the first job of AA Command that much easier – the prevention of accurate bombing.

The 4.5in. HAA gun was a superb weapon, although its heavy weight meant it was only available for static emplacements. By January 1941 London was defended by 72 guns, followed by the naval base at Scapa Flow with 32 and the shipbuilding yards on the Tyne also with 32. The primary purpose of the distinctive shielding around the gun was to protect the crew from the powerful back-blast when the weapon was fired. (IWM)

TYPES OF HAA GUN ENGAGEMENT

AA Command employed three methods of fire control against high-flying Luftwaffe bombers – continuously pointed fire, predicted

HAA Battery

The layout plan for a typical AA Command four-gun 3.7in. fixed HAA site at the beginning of the war. These early sites lacked full permanent building structures and relied on earthwork or sandbagged enclosures for the command post and targeting instruments. Each four-gun site was manned by 80 men, but not all had permanent living quarters like those depicted here, forcing many gunners to live near their weapons under canvas in all weathers.

1. 3.7in. gun emplacements
2. Roadway
3. Predictor No. 1 Mk III
4. Command post
5. No. 1 Mk IV height-finder
6. Magazines
7. Gun store
8. Living quarters
9. Sentry/Military Police quarters
10. Fence
11. Main road

concentration fire and box barrage fire. Continuously pointed fire was the most dangerous type, and it relied on good visual or gun laying radar acquisition of the target formation. This type of fire was designed to place shells directly in front of the lead aircraft in the formation, the gunners expending a continuous pattern of bursts along the bomber's course. Each battery would maintain pointed fire until the formation was no longer in range, new batteries then taking over.

Predicted concentration fire was less effective than continuously pointed fire. It was used at night, through cloud or when radar information was of low quality. Gunners fired short barrages at points in the sky through which it was predicted the target aircraft would pass.

Least effective was box barrage fire, which was also the most wasteful type of AA fire. Used at night or when cloud prevented good visual aiming, it was designed to put as many shells as possible into a certain area of sky known as 'the box', which was hopefully located just ahead of the expected bomb release line of the incoming formation. If 'the box' was properly placed, Luftwaffe bombers had no choice but to fly through it. During the Blitz it was called the 'London Barrage'.

For low-level defence, AA Command employed the superb 40mm Bofors autocannon. Design of this weapon began in Sweden in 1930, and seven years later the British Army placed an order for 100 guns. Shortly thereafter, licence production was agreed and more guns were manufactured in Britain for both the British Army and the Royal Navy. The Bofors was air cooled and fired a two-pound impact-fused explosive shell to an effective range of 6,000ft. The rate of fire was 120 rounds per minute, and a single hit usually meant the end of any bomber or fighter caught at low-level.

During the Battle of Britain, AA Command had just 366 Bofors guns available, with most if not all assigned to the most valuable targets – radar stations, airfields (where the LAA batteries were manned by RAF personnel) and factories. These sites were categorised as Vital (later Vulnerable) Point (VP) targets. Radar stations were protected by three or four Bofors guns, with some sites (including Pevensey CH) also being defended by Hispano-Suiza Mk 1 20mm cannon. The largest number deployed at one site was eight, these weapons ringing the joint HQ of RAF Fighter Command and AA Command at Stanmore.

The most numerous LAA weapon in AA Command's arsenal was the World War I-era 0.303in. machine gun. Gas-operated, the Lewis gun had a rate of fire of between 500–600 rounds a minute. Pre-war estimates for effective airfield defence required 16 40mm Bofors and eight HAA guns. The lack of the former meant most airfields were defended by multiple Lewis guns in single, double and quadruple mountings. By the summer of 1940, the airfields of Nos. 10 and 11 Group around London and to the west of the capital were identified as being the most vulnerable to air attack, and they

The 40mm Bofors gun was the best LAA weapon of the war. During the Battle of Britain, gunners manning Bofors took aim through open sights as seen here. The Bofors was fed by four-round clips, and after the first shot was rammed and fired, the weapon kept firing two shots every second until the loader stopped dropping clips into the feed tray. A single hit from a two-pound HE impact-fused shell fired by a Bofors gun was usually sufficient to bring down an aircraft. This particular weapon defended an RAF Fighter Command airfield in No. 11 Group in 1940. (Andy Saunders Collection)

duly received a mix bag of weapons. These included 40mm Bofors, veteran 3in. guns and Lewis guns. Searchlight and AA batteries were equipped with a single Lewis gun for defence.

To contest night raids, AA batteries worked with a network of searchlights and individual sound locators. At the outbreak of war and in the first months of the Blitz, AA gunners relied on them when cloud or darkness concealed enemy aircraft. In theory, the sound locators would listen for approaching bombers and be able to provide searchlights with their approximate range and height. When a bomber was found and 'coned' by several searchlights, the guns would engage. In practice, the sound locators added little to the defence and were easily swamped by several bombers flying in different directions at once.

During the summer of 1940, the 120cm SL projector type rated at 210 million candle power was the most common searchlight in service with the Royal Artillery. As the Blitz intensified, the 150cm 510 million candlepower searchlight became more widely available following its entry into service just prior to the outbreak of war. Searchlights were not especially successful at helping AA Command destroy enemy aircraft.

GUN LAYING RADAR

By the summer of 1940, AA Command had roughly 300 Gun Laying (GL) Mk I radar sets in service. They could identify an aircraft's range accurately, but azimuth measurements were imprecise and they could not measure elevation. The Mk I was more of a 'gun assisting radar', for it was incapable of directing AA fire with any degree of accuracy. While limited, the Mk I did provide AA gunners with the chance to gain experience of working with radar, preparing them for when vastly improved Mk II units became operational in early 1941. The Mk II produced more accurate azimuth and elevation information, improving gunners' accuracy at night.

SLC radar was also added to AA Command's network of searchlight batteries. Codenamed 'Elsie', individual units were fitted directly onto searchlights, giving them a maximum range of eight miles when searching for a bomber-sized aircraft. The new radar enabled the operator to align the searchlight on the target aircraft before having to switch it on. It also made it easier to hold the beam on the aircraft during evasive manoeuvres.

KB barrage balloons were designed to deter accurate attacks by dive-bombers, low-level medium bombers and fighter-bombers. Tethered at heights of up to 15,000ft, these barrages proved effective. They were also sporting targets for roaming Bf 109 pilots. (Author's Collection)

BARRAGE BALLOON

Compared to the modern and fast Ju 88, the simple barrage balloon seemed like an archaic leftover from another war, but it played an important role. Overseen by RAF Barrage Balloon Command, headquartered at Stanmore, the barrage balloon was the last link in the ground defences.

Located over important targets, the standard hydrogen-filled KB barrage balloon flew at a maximum height of 15,000ft. Like the guns, they forced incoming raiders to fly at higher altitudes. This degraded bombing accuracy and allowed aircraft to be engaged by HAA guns in the target area. Balloons could also bring aircraft down. If a bomber hit the balloon's cable, the drag generated would cause the aircraft to stall and crash – unless its wings were fitted with balloon fenders to slice through the cable. During the entire war, barrage balloons were credited with destroying just 30 enemy aircraft.

In July 1940, AA Command had 1,466 balloons available out of a nominal establishment of 1,865. For all their antiquity, there is no record of any low-flying German bomber, fighter-bomber or dive-bomber making a deliberate attack on a facility protected by a balloon barrage.

SITING GUNS

The speed and range of the Luftwaffe's medium bombers meant they could attack targets throughout Britain from almost any direction. To properly protect vulnerable targets, AA guns were deployed to provide all-round cover. A typical pin-point target like a munitions factory or airfield required at least four HAA gun troops of four weapons each. These batteries were sited in a square pattern around the target about one mile from it.

Luftwaffe bombing tactics included dive-bombing, low-level bomber/fighter-bomber attacks and, most commonly, high-altitude pattern bombing attacks. As the bombers approached, formations were tightened for the run on the target, with the crews' focus turning to the lead bomber. In the latter aircraft, the lead bomb-aimer directed the flight path of both his aircraft and the rest of the formation. The second he released his bombs, the rest of the formation followed. This resulted in a bombing pattern that created both hits and misses, but hopefully enough of the former to be effective.

To counter this tactic, AA gunners targeted the

Luftwaffe bomber formations were designed to offer the best mutual fire support from multiple machine guns to protect themselves from fighter attack. To minimise the dangers of HAA fire, Luftwaffe bombers used speed (180mph) and height (16,000ft) through the target zone as their best defence. Bombers were most vulnerable to HAA fire during the final 90 seconds before bomb release. RAF fighter pilots quickly learned not to chase bombers that were being targeted by HAA fire, instead waiting to attack those solitary aircraft forced from the relative safety of their formations due to shrapnel damage.

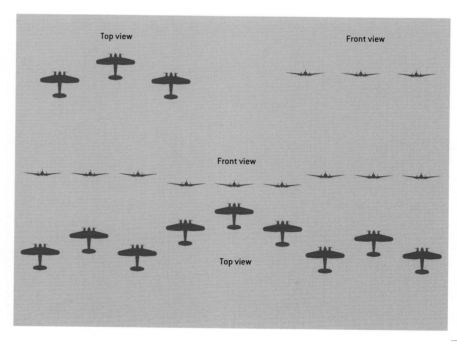

Top view   Front view

Front view

Top view

17

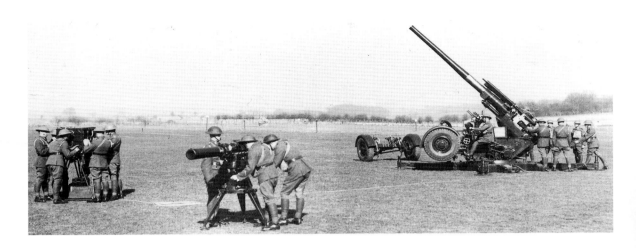

The 3.7in. gun was the mainstay of Britain's HAA defences throughout the war. It fired 28lb HE shells at a rate of ten per minute. Here, the gun is shown with its associated Stroud No. 1 Mk IV height-finder (centre) and Vickers-Armstrongs Predictor No. 1 Mk III (left). The normal deployment was in a half-battery of four guns, using targeting information from the same height-finder and predictor. Since the gun sites were themselves liable to come under air attack, protective walls of sandbags or concrete usually surrounded the height-finder, predictor and individual guns. (IWM)

OPPOSITE

The QF 3.7in. mobile HAA gun was the most important heavy weapon of its type in service with AA Command during the Battle of Britain/Blitz. Its mobility meant the gun could be moved quickly to adjust to changing Luftwaffe targeting and tactics. In action, the riggers would be dropped and levelled to provide a stable firing platform. In terms of AA performance, the 3.7in. weapon was just as good as the deadly German 88mm FlaK series, the American M1 90mm and the Italian Canonone da 90/53 90mm AA guns of World War II.

formation leader's aircraft. Against a bomber formation flying at 16,000ft, the 3.7in. HAA gun had a maximum range of five-and-a-half miles. The limit of the gun engagement zone was, therefore, the circumference of a near circle of six-and-a-half miles centred on the target – the five-and-a-half miles range of the gun, plus the one mile separation between the gun sites and the target. As the raiding force approached the target, and while still outside the range of the 3.7in. weapons, the height-finder and predictor operators at each gun site tracked the leading aircraft and the gunners trained their weapons on the predicted aiming point ahead of it.

Once past the six-and-a-half-mile circle, the attacking formation would come under fire from the nearest gun site. As the lead aircraft began its run, all four batteries had the bomber's range and would open fire with continuously aimed predicted fire.

Bombs released from 16,000ft at 180mph had a forward throw of about one-and-a-half miles, meaning ordnance dropped at that height travelled that distance and marked the line of bomb release. Once across that line, and following bomb release, the bombers were no longer a threat. If another formation followed, fire would be quickly shifted onto it and the process repeated. If it was only a one-formation attack, AA gunners would continue to fire for as long as possible. Once free of their bombs, aircraft quickly loosened formation, increased their speed, changed altitude and turned away from the target. This overwhelmed the predictors and greatly reduced accuracy.

For low-level attacks, siting the 40mm Bofors guns was even more problematic. Fighter-bombers were the most difficult to engage. They were fast (300mph), and when attacking targets without ample warning, they gave gunners very little time to engage them. Fired over open sights, the Bofors gun was most effective against aircraft flying directly towards or directly away from it. The gunners' aim was greatly assisted by the Kerrison Director, this mechanical analogue computer being one of the first fully automated AA fire-control systems to achieve operational service. Driving gun laying electrically, it was developed by Maj A. V. Kerrison of the British Army. These directors were in short supply during the battle, forcing gunners to use their iron sites when firing.

Fighter-bombers typically released their bomb in a shallow dive from 600ft, giving the ordnance a forward throw of about half-a-mile from the target. A Bofors gun had a maximum effective range of just over a mile, meaning it could engage a target if

VICKERS-ARMSTRONGS QF 3.7in. HAA GUN (MOBILE)

spotted early, and before the aircraft began a diving attack. It was critical for the guns to be positioned so they covered the raiders' likely approach routes. Once the latter had been identified, the guns were positioned for the best chance of success. The shortage of Bofors autocannon in 1940–41 meant there were never enough to provide protection from every possible direction.

ELECTRONIC COUNTER MEASURES

Before the Blitz began in earnest, the RAF Wireless Interception Unit discovered *Knickebein* signals in June 1940. Although this was a relatively simple two-beam radio target marking system that allowed suitably equipped aircraft to blind-bomb targets at night or in poor weather, its existence sent a chill through RAF Intelligence. When briefed on the situation, Prime Minister Churchill ordered the formation of a radio counter-measures unit as the highest priority. On 7 October the unit was renamed No. 80 Wing, under the command of Wg Cdr Edward Addison and controlled directly by the Air Ministry.

Purpose-built jammers known as 'Aspirins' (to counter *Knickebein* beams, codenamed 'Headaches' by the RAF) were soon made ready by the Telecommunications Research Establishment at Swanage, in Dorest, but their success was limited. One of the Battle of Britain/Blitz myths has it that No. 80 Wing 'bent the beams', forcing the Germans to stop using the system in the early stages of the Blitz. In reality, Luftwaffe crews could still detect the beams despite the jamming, with the advent of 'Aspirin' sets confirming that the RAF was aware of *Knickebein*. This created a level of anxiety amongst bomber crews, and the belief that RAF nightfighters could use the detection of active *Knickebein* to 'hunt in the beam'. This was not true, but consequently there was a reluctance by crews to use the equipment over Britain.

DESPERATE WEAPONS

The shortage of AA guns for airfield defence forced the British Army to develop some stopgap devices that, while innovative, were short lived with limited success. The first was the Parachute And Cable (PAC) system, with launchers consisting of a small rocket trailing a steel cable. The 480ft length of steel cable was suspended beneath a parachute, which opened automatically when the rocket reached its optimal height of 600ft. The rockets were grouped in batteries of nine and were situated at sites on the perimeter of an aerodrome.

The rockets were launched as a single salvo, creating a curtain of steel cables across the path of a low-flying aircraft. When an aircraft struck the cable and started to carry it forwards, the jolt of the impact caused the opening of a second drag chute attached at the bottom end of the cable. If snagged on a wing or any other part of an aircraft, the added drag from the two parachutes induced a violent and rapid deceleration that was sufficient to cause the aircraft to stall and crash.

By July 1940, 26 airfields and industrial sites were equipped with PAC systems. During 1940–41, it was only successfully fired twice. The PAC system's greatest achievement occurred on 18 August when nine Do 17s of 9./KG 76 made a low-level attack on Kenley airfield in Surrey. One aircraft was brought down by the cables and two damaged. The only other success occurred on 18 February 1941, when a He 111 from KG 53 was brought down by a PAC at Watton airfield, Norfolk.

The other rocket system that was introduced – in early 1941 – was the Unrotated Projectile, UP for short. These 3in. rockets were 6ft 4in. long, weighed 54lb and carried a 22lb warhead fused to explode at a pre-set time after launch. Once fired, each rocket accelerated to 1,000mph in one-and-a-half seconds and then coasted to its maximum altitude of 19,000ft. A single battery could launch a salvo of 128 rockets to produce a 'shot gun' effect. As a one-shot weapon, UP was inaccurate, which meant that it was not deployed in large numbers.

Just like the UP and PAC systems, there was no air defence idea that was too outlandish to consider. One such concept was the 'aerial minefield'. Using what was officially known as the Long Aerial Mine, RAF aircraft would drop a string of mines into the path of incoming bombers. These mines weighed 14lb and were housed in a small cylindrical drum. Once released, the mine, with a one pound warhead, was slowed by a parachute. Attached to the base of the warhead was 2,000ft of piano wire, with a second packed parachute at the bottom end.

When an aircraft struck the piano wire, the shock of the impact was enough to release the larger upper parachute. Once free, a smaller parachute unfurled, which stabilised the bomb in its fall. The initial impact also triggered a parachute at the bottom of the wire. The larger lower parachute then pulled down the upper bomb, which exploded on contact with the aircraft.

Laying a curtain of Long Aerial Mines required a bomber flying at 20,000ft. The aircraft chosen for this job was the obsolete Handley Page Harrow, modified to carry 120 mines. Once at altitude, the Harrow would release its mines at 200ft intervals at right angles to the track of incoming bombers. This slowly descending barrier was four-and-a-half miles long and nearly half-a-mile deep.

In December 1940, No. 93 Sqn was formed at Burtonwood, in Cheshire, and issued with Harrows to begin aerial mining operations. The only recorded success occurred on the night of 22 December, when a Harrow laid a string of mines in front of two German bombers as they approached the coast. One was subsequently assessed as having been destroyed. On 13 March 1941, another German bomber was claimed as 'probably' destroyed. Aerial mining was not a success, and in November 1941 the scheme was abandoned.

PASSIVE DEFENCE

During the Blitz an important part of AA Command's air defences were dummy airfields and decoy fire sites. The latter were codenamed Starfish and were designed to create the illusion of a city under air attack. A Starfish comprised a cluster of fires located in open country at least four miles from the target it was intended to protect. By March 1941, 108 Starfish sites were operational around Britain. These sites proved to be somewhat successful, at times fooling German bombers to drop their loads onto empty fields.

These 4.5in. guns, sited at Mudchute on the Isle of Dogs, were assigned to the 154th Battery of the 52nd (London) HAA Regiment. Heavy rescue worker Bill Regan lived near to the battery (which was originally equipped with 3.7in. guns). In March 1941, he wrote in his diary, 'They have four big AA guns installed, and they used them last night, and what a lovely sound. They go off as one, we can hear the scream as they go up, and follow the sound, and they explode together, forming a square, and if the aim is right, it's got to be curtains for the aeroplane on the end of it'. (Andy Saunders Collection)

LUFTWAFFE BOMBERS

A He 111P delivers its payload of vertically stowed SC 250 bombs during the Battle of France. Heinkel's medium bomber was a mainstay of the Luftwaffe's day and night assault on Britain in 1940–41, having first seen action during the Spanish Civil War. (Andy Saunders Collection)

On 10 August 1940, the Luftwaffe Quartermaster General's returns showed that 3,358 aircraft were available for combat against Britain. Of that total, 2,593 were serviceable. This worked out to 998 medium bombers, 261 dive-bombers, 195 reconnaissance aircraft, 80 maritime aircraft and 30 Bf 109/Bf 110 *Jabo* fighter-bombers. The rest was made up of 805 single-seat and 224 two-seat fighters. While the numbers are impressive, it also reveals a force that was not growing in strength.

At the beginning of the western campaign on 10 May 1940, the Luftwaffe had 1,771 medium bombers, but within two months this figure had dropped to 1,482 ready for the Battle of Britain. The unexpected attrition rates during the conquest of France meant the Luftwaffe was barely keeping pace with replacement aircraft and crews.

The He 111 was the Luftwaffe's first purpose-designed, modern twin-engined medium bomber. The prototype took to the air for the first time on 24 February 1935, after which flight chief test pilot Gerhard Nitschke was full of praise for the new bomber. It was fast, with very good flight and landing characteristics, stability during cruising and descent and adequate single-engine performance. At the end of 1935 three more prototypes entered flight-testing, with the He 111A-1 prototype flying on 10 January 1936. It made headlines by becoming the 'fastest passenger aircraft in the world' with a top speed exceeding 249mph.

In the autumn of 1936, the prototype He 111B made its maiden flight, with the first production model rolling off the assembly line later that same year. Powered by Daimler-Benz DB 600C engines driving variable-pitch propellers, the He 111B-0 could carry 3,306lb of ordnance in a vertical bomb-bay or mines externally. Some 300 He 111B-1s were ordered, with the first being delivered to the Luftwaffe in January 1937. Just two months later the He 111 made its combat debut during the Spanish Civil War. As part of the *Legion Condor*, four B-1s attacked Republican airfields in support of Nationalist forces during the Battle of Guadalajara in March 1937.

Capable of carrying a heavier bombload than any of its contemporaries then in frontline service, the He 111P/H was the Luftwaffe's standard medium bomber by July 1940. It equipped 15 of 33 *Kampfgruppen* based on the Channel coast for the Battle of Britain/Blitz.

In August 1935, the *Reichsluftfahrtministerium* (RLM – German Air Ministry) issued a requirement for an unarmed, three-seat high-speed bomber with a bombload of 1,763–2,204lb. In response, Junkers submitted its Ju 88 design. In June 1936 the RLM ordered two prototypes, the V1 and V2. Three further prototypes followed, all powered by a pair of Jumo 211 engines and capable of a 1,242-mile range.

The Ju 88 V1 made its first flight on 21 December 1936. A top speed of 360mph was achieved, delighting Generalfeldmarschall Hermann Göring. Here was the Luftwaffe's high-speed *Schnellbomber* (fast bomber) that could outrun the fighters of the period. In March 1939 the fifth prototype set a 621-mile closed circuit record with a 4,409lb payload, clocking a speed of 321mph. As impressive as these numbers were, *Generalluftzeugmeister* Ernst Udet, the Luftwaffe's director of research and development, also ordered the development of the Ju 88 as a heavy dive-bomber. This occurred in October 1937, and the directive effectively marked the beginning of the end of the Ju 88 as a *Schnellbomber*. By 1938 the aircraft had been radically modified, with its fuselage being lengthened, wings strengthened and dive brakes added, and the crew increased to four.

As a dive-bomber, the Ju 88 was capable of delivering heavy loads with great accuracy. However, this came at a high cost, for the stresses and strains associated with dive-bombing proved too much for the airframe. Later in the war, the dive angle was changed to a shallower 45 degrees, allowing for the removal of the dive brakes.

Due to development problems, production was badly delayed, resulting in the first Ju 88s not entering service until 1 September 1939 – the day Germany invaded Poland. Manufacturing rates improved painfully slowly, with Junkers producing just one Ju 88 per week. Despite the aircraft being the Luftwaffe's most capable and versatile bomber, there were just 12 *Gruppen* fully equipped in August 1940.

Like the Ju 88, the Do 17 was ordered as a 'high-speed aircraft with a twin tail'. In 1932, the *Heereswaffenamt* (Ordnance Department) called for a 'freight aircraft for the German State Railway' and a high-speed mail aeroplane for *Deutsche Lufthansa*'. The civilian descriptions were to hide the fact that this aircraft was destined to be used as a bomber, in direct contravention of the Treaty of Versailles.

On 17 March 1933, the RLM gave Dornier the go ahead to build several Do 17 prototypes. Their production commenced on 20 May 1934, with the first prototype

A trio of early Ju 88A-1s from a training unit. The snow on the ground would suggest that these are aircraft of *Lehrgruppe* 88, photographed in the winter of 1939–40 at the unit's Greifswald home. Formed in November 1939 to train new crews destined to fly the Ju 88 operationally, *Lehrgruppe* 88 was redesignated *Ergänzungskampfgruppe* 4 in March 1940. (Tony Holmes Collection)

Ju 88A-1 Wk-Nr 4136 3Z+BB of *Stab* I./KG 77, Laon-Athies, France, October 1940

Flown by Oberleutnant Siegward Fiebeg, 3Z+BB crashed in flames near Eastend Green Farm at Hertingfordbury, Hertfordshire, after being hit by LAA fire on 3 October 1940 during a low-level attack on the de Havilland aircraft works adjoining Hatfield aerodrome. The aircraft was hit in both engines by 40mm shells fired by Bofors guns and 0.303in. rounds fired by Lewis machine guns. Although the four-man crew survived, the attack killed 21 people and injured 70, disrupting work on the Mosquito prototype.

(V1, with a single vertical stabiliser) flying on 23 November that same year. The twin-tailed V2 took to the air on 18 May 1935. After both aircraft had been evaluated by the RLM, the V1 was retrofitted with a twin tail due to the latter design offering better stability. The V3, also with a twin tail and powered by two BMW VI 7.3 engines, flew for the first time on 19 September 1935. Four more prototypes followed, with the final V9, ironically, being tested as a high-speed airliner.

The first production variant was the Do 17E-1, powered by two Daimler-Benz DB 600 engines, and the Do 17F-1 reconnaissance version fitted with two BMW VI engines.

Luftwaffe units began converting to the new aircraft in early 1937, and by July 1940 the Do 17Z bomber and, in smaller numbers, the Do 17P reconnaissance aircraft were in service powered by Bramo-Fafnir 323 radial engines.

The Do 17 was primarily used as a short-range battlefield interdiction and airfield attack bomber. Although considered obsolete by July 1940, Do 17Zs still equipped eight *Kampfgruppen* at the start of the Battle of Britain. Amongst those units was KG 3, whose II. *Gruppe* flew this aircraft. (Getty)

The Dornier's light bombload and short range made it the least effective of the Luftwaffe's three bombers. Nevertheless, in July 1940, the aircraft equipped eight *Kampfgruppen*. Production of the Do 17Z ended in September, from which point the aircraft was slowly replaced on the channel front by the Ju 88.

The Ju 87B is arguably the most recognised Luftwaffe aircraft of World War II. Its gestation period was far longer than the He 111, Ju 88 and Do 17, the aircraft being able to trace its origins back as far as

1929 and the Junkers K 47. Designed as a two-seat fighter, the K 47 was found to be capable of carrying a 220lb bomb load. Three airframes were tested in the dive-bombing role. Although a highly capable precision bomber, the K 47 was expensive to build and no further examples were completed. The seeds had been sown, however.

Design work on the Ju 87 began in 1933, and two years later the construction of three prototypes was well underway. The prototype Ju 87 V1, which had a twin-tail unit and was powered by a Rolls-Royce Kestrel V engine, flew for the first time on 17 September 1935. The aircraft suffered tail failure on 24 January 1936 and crashed, killing Junkers' chief test pilot, Willy Neuenhofen, and his engineer, Heinrich Kreft. The remaining prototypes, and all production aircraft, were built with a centrally mounted single fin and rudder.

At the end of 1936, the first Ju 87A-O pre-production models started coming off the production line. These were followed by the first A-1/2 production aircraft in 1937. By the start of World War II, the Ju 87A had been withdrawn from frontline

Ju 87B-1 Wk-Nr 5227 6G+KS of 5./StG 1, Saint-Omer, France, November 1940

On 18 August 1940, StG 77 had 18 Ju 87s shot down or written off, finally ending the Stuka's participation in the Battle of Britain. And when Operation *Seelöwe* was quietly shelved on Hitler's orders, the bulk of the *Stukagruppen* were transferred back to Germany. A number of *Staffeln* did remain in northern France, and on 1 November 27 Ju 87Bs from StG 1 mounted a raid on shipping in the Straits of Dover and Thames Estuary. The Stukas sank three vessels, but Ju 87B-1 6G+KS, crewed by pilot Gefreiter Werner Karrath and wireless operator/gunner Gefreiter Max Aulehner, was shot down by Royal Navy AA fire. Although Karrath was killed in the crash, Aulehner was rescued by a British motor torpedo boat.

service and replaced by the considerably improved Ju 87B-1. Powered by a Junkers Jumo 211Da engine that developed 1,200hp for take-off, the B-model could carry a 1,543lb bomb load. During 1939, 557 Ju 87B-1s came off the assembly lines, and by December of that year the B-2 had replaced the B-1 in production. Equipped with an improved wooden propeller with broader blades, the B-2 could lift a maximum bomb load of 2,205lb – the same as the internal load carried by the Do 17Z.

To increase the Stuka's range, the Ju 87R was developed in parallel with the B-2. Built in reasonably large numbers, the R-model was fitted with an additional 32-gallon fuel tank in each outer wing section and plumbing for two wing-mounted 65-gallon (300-litre) drop tanks. These increased the aircraft's range to 869 miles, double that of the Ju 87B-2. By August 1940, seven *Gruppen* of Ju 87B-2s and three of Ju 87Rs were ready for action.

On 1 July 1940, the Luftwaffe's first dedicated fighter-bomber unit was formed. Designated ErprGr 210, it was equipped with modified versions of both the Bf 109 and Bf 110. The primary fighter-bomber version of the Bf 109E was the E-4/B *Jagdbomber* (*Jabo*), although examples of the E-1/B and E-7/B also bombed targets in southeast England from September 1940. The aircraft could be equipped with an ETC 500 weapon rack mounted between the wheels for a 551lb bomb, or an ETC 50 rack for four 110lb bombs. The addition of bomb racks reduced the Bf 109E's speed by less than five miles per hour, but the presence of ordnance increased this figure to 12.5mph.

The Bf 110D-0/B was the first fighter-bomber variant of Messerschmitt's much vaunted, but ultimately disappointing, *Zerstörer* (Destroyer). The D-model was fitted with ETC 250 bomb racks housed in a rectangular fairing mounted on the centre fuselage just beneath the cockpit. Capable of carrying two 1,102lb bombs, and armed with two 20mm Oerlikon MG FF cannon and four 7.92mm machine guns, the Bf 110D-0/B was a formidable ground attack aircraft.

At the beginning of August 1940, ErprGr 210 had just 30 Bf 109E-4/Bs and Bf 110-0/Ds serviceable. While the unit managed to achieve some stunning successes despite its paucity in numbers, ErprGr 210 also suffered heavy losses during the Battle of Britain.

Encouraged by the unit's precision attacks and dismayed by the losses being suffered by his medium bomber units, Generalfeldmarschall Göring instructed each *Jagdgeschwadern* on 4 September to convert a single *Staffel* per *Jagdgruppe* into a dedicated *Jabo* unit. This significant change in tactics put even more pressure on already stretched AA Command batteries in southeast England.

BOMBS AND BOMB AIMING

During the Battle of Britain and the Blitz the Luftwaffe deployed four main categories of bombs. The most frequently used was the *Sprengbombe-Cylindrisch* (SC or explosive bomb, cylindrical), which initially came in three weights – 110lb, 551lb and 2,204lb. Higher capacity and heavier versions were introduced later in the campaign, including the SC 1000, SC 1800 'Satan', SC 2000 and SC 2500 'Max'.

By mid-September 1940, some Luftwaffe units had begun dropping the high-capacity *Spezialbombe* (SB) 1000 anti-shipping *Luftmine* adopted for land use. Dropped by parachute, these weapons were impossible to aim with any degree of accuracy.

The smallest and most effective weapon used in 1940–41 was the humble 2.2lb B1E1 *Elektronbrandbombe* (electron incendiary bomb). Designed to start fires, they could generate enough heat to melt steel. With 36 B1E1s packed into BSK *Schuttkasten* ('hopper') cluster bomb containers, a single bomber could scatter several hundred over a single target.

To reduce exposure to anti-aircraft fire, Luftwaffe medium bombers flew at between 13,000–16,000ft. However, from these altitudes the Zeiss-Jena *Lofte* C/7D *Lofternrohr* (vertical telescope) bombsight was not an accurate device. Tests in 1937 showed that Do 17 and He 111 bomb aimers were able to put just two per cent of their bombs within a

Luftwaffe groundcrew, known as 'black men' due to the colour of their overalls, prepare to load the second of two SC 1000 2,000lb bombs to external racks fitted to a suitably camouflaged He 111H during the Blitz. The armourers leaning over the bomb are setting its fuze. (Tony Holmes Collection)

SC 250 Bomb

The 551lb *Sprengbombe-Cylindrisch* (SC, explosive bomb, cylindrical) 250 was the Luftwaffe's most widely used bomb during the Battle of Britain. Its body was 46.2in. long, and overall length increased to 65in. with the inclusion of the tail. The bomb had a diameter of 14.5in. There were many explosive fillings for the weapon, all weighing 276lb. The He 111P/H could carry eight SC 250s internally, while the Ju 88A was capable of carrying four internally and four externally.

600ft radius around the target. When exposed to accurate AA fire, the bomb aimers' miss distance was multiplied three-fold. The Ju 87 force, however, remained clinically accurate even when opposed by ground fire. Enemy fighters proved to be its nemesis.

NAVIGATION, BLIND BOMBING AND PATHFINDERS

During the Spanish Civil War, medium bomber crews of the *Legion Condor* grappled with the problem of finding a target at night or in poor weather. Shortly after *Luftflotten* 2 and 3 moved into their new airfields in France, Belgium and the Netherlands in the summer of 1940, preparations for the coming battle included the speedy fielding of a comprehensive ground-based navigation system. These electronic aids were divided into three categories, namely navigation, blind landing and target marking for blind bombing.

In the late 1920s and early 1930s, C. Lorenz AG of Berlin developed a blind-landing system that was capable of guiding an aircraft to all but the most fog-shrouded airfield. The system, suitably christened *Lorenz* after its manufacturer, consisted of two adjacent transmitters that emitted a pair of beams up to a range of 30 miles. The beams were made up of Morse dots (left) and dashes (right). When the two beams overlapped in the middle, they formed a continuous note or equifinal. With the note established, the pilot knew his aircraft was on course for the runway. This revolutionised airline service, and was also employed by the RAF and emerging Luftwaffe.

Knickebein was produced by the Telefunken company and was a relatively simple method of marking targets with a pair of radio beams. As one beam guided the aircraft to the target, much like the *Lorenz* beam, a second beam would cross over the first, marking the bomb release point. While the system worked well, it was limited by range – a bomber flying at 20,000ft could bomb a target 270 miles away with a fair degree of accuracy. In practice, however, Luftwaffe bombers rarely reached that height in 1940. The narrowness of the approach beam also caused problems for crews. At just one-third of a degree in width, it meant the beam was just one mile wide at a distance of 180 miles. Accurate bombing proved to be all but impossible, and as RAF countermeasures increased, many crews used *Knickebein* for navigation only and bombed visually once they had reached their target.

X-Gerät (Apparatus), which succeeded *Knickebein*, used six separate beams emitted from ground stations in German-occupied territory. Three approach beams, two fine

and one course, were aimed directly at the target. Three cross-beams intersected the approach beams at various distances from the target. At 30 miles from the aiming point, the first cross-beam would provide the first course correction. At 12 miles from bomb release, the second course beam would be crossed and any course changes made. As the bomber flew through the third cross-beam, a timed bomb run would begin. *X-Gerät* was the most advanced system of its type in the world at the time, and it required a high degree of skill and training to be effective.

Using just a single beam, *Y-Gerät* was the third, and most sophisticated, bomb aiming device employed by the Luftwaffe. Outbound bombers received the beam's signal, which was returned by a transponder back to the beam station. Using the radar method of calculating an aircraft's range (distance = speed x time), the bomber's distance from the station and, therefore, the distance to the target was established. Upon reaching the bomb-release point, the bomber was sent a signal and ordnance dropped.

These three radio beam systems gave the Luftwaffe bombers a distinct advantage, allowing them to attack general area targets at night and in bad weather with a fair degree of accuracy. They were not accurate enough for pin-point bombing, however.

Not all bombers could be equipped and their crews specially trained to use the *X-Gerät* and *Y-Gerät* systems. In November 1939, KGr 100 was formed as the primary target-marking pathfinder force. As sophisticated as the beam navigation and blind bombing systems were, the actual target marking by KGr 100 was crude and largely ineffective. The *Fallschirmleuchtbombe* LC50F (parachute illumination bomb) and the B1E1 incendiary bomb were lightweight weapons and tended to drift in the wind, sometimes miles from their intended target. Even with the correct bomb release point, the actual marked aiming point could be off by hundreds of feet.

Luftwaffe night bombing tactics ranged from single aircraft to mass raids by several hundred. For the Blitz campaign, the most widely used tactic was the continuous attack in which bombers from across France, Belgium and the Netherlands would attack a target over an extended period of time – raids could last as long as nine hours. This put a great deal of strain on the AA defences, with the expenditure of thousands of shells for only modest results.

The *Dreimaster* (Three-master) He 111Hs of KGr 100 were easily identifiable, as they were fitted with three dorsal-mounted antennas that denoted the unit's specialist pathfinder/target marking role. Even with some of the most advanced electronic navigation equipment then in service, Luftwaffe target marking during the Blitz was crude and largely ineffective. (Chris Goss Collection)

TECHNICAL SPECIFICATIONS

BRITISH AA DEFENCES

VICKERS-ARMSTRONGS QF 3.7in.

The most numerous HAA gun deployed by AA Command in the summer of 1940 was the 3.7in. weapon. The first prototype appeared in 1936, but its initial development was so slow that pilot pre-production models only commenced development trials with the British Army in January 1938. The new gun was an extremely advanced design for its time, receiving aiming information electrically from the predictor on dial pointers. All the gunners had to do was operate the weapon's controls so that the dial pointers were continuously matched, while the rest of the crew loaded and fired.

The 3.7in. was produced as both a mobile unit (Mk I) and a static gun (Mk II). With a muzzle velocity of 2,600ft per second, it could fire a 28lb high explosive (HE) shell to an effective ceiling of 25,000ft. Maximum firing ranges were 3.5 miles horizontally and 7.5 miles when at a slant. A typical gun crew comprised 11 men – No. 1 NCO gun commander, No. 2 layer for bearing, No. 3 layer for elevation, No. 4 shell fuze setter, No. 5-breach loader and six 'ammunition numbers'.

VICKERS-ARMSTRONGS QF 4.5in.

The 4.5in. HAA gun had a long gestation period. In the late 1920s and early 1930s, the British Army was developing a 4.7in. weapon. Production priorities for the 3.7in.

OPPOSITE
In 1940, the 4.5in. HAA gun was fitted with an electric rammer (as seen here) that allowed it to fire eight rounds per minute. Being a heavy weapon, it was a static AA gun, although it could be moved on a special Transporting Limber. AA Command had to rely on its limited supply of 3.7in. mobile guns to meet changing Luftwaffe targeting and tactics. (IWM)

gun meant there was little chance for the 4.7in. weapon to emerge. The Royal Navy's 4.5in. gun was already in production, and it was adopted by the British Army to replace the 4.7in. weapon. While the Admiralty agreed to divert some of its production to the British Army, it was only on the understanding that the guns be used for the defence of naval installations.

The gun was fitted with an open back, mild steel shield and equipped with a power rammer, a heavy counterweight over the breach and a fuze setter on the loading tray. It fired a 54lb HE shell to an effective ceiling of 26,000ft. Muzzle velocity was 2,400ft per second, with a rate of fire of eight rounds per minute.

ORDNANCE QF 3in. 20cwt

A leftover from World War I, the 3in. 20cwt HAA gun had a reasonable performance, but it lacked the power of newer weapons and was due for replacement by 1939. One of the first guns designed for anti-aircraft use, it had a simple layout featuring a barrel and recuperator/recoil mechanism slung between two side mounting plates carried on a turntable. During the 1930s, and prior to the outbreak of war, the 3in. 20cwt was updated, and many gunners preferred it to the heavier and more complex 3.7in. weapon. Firing a 16lb shell at a muzzle velocity of 2,000ft per second, it had an effective ceiling of 16,000ft.

BOFORS Mk I

When the Battle of Britain began the 40mm Bofors Mk I was the finest LAA gun in the world. Produced by AB Bofors of Sweden, the first model appeared in 1929. As the British Army looked for a viable LAA weapon to replace the unsatisfactory Vickers 40mm Pom-Pom gun, it turned to AB Bofors. After a series of demonstrations in the mid 1930s, the British Army placed an order in April 1937 for 100 L/60 1936 guns and 50,000 rounds of ammunition. This was quickly followed by a manufacturing licence agreement, allowing production to begin in Britain.

Unfortunately for AA Command, it not only had to prepare for war against the Luftwaffe but also fight an interservice battle with the Royal Navy for resources. At the beginning of the conflict many of AA Command's 253 Bofors guns (against a requirement for 1,860 to properly defend vital targets) were actually on loan

3.7in. HAA Shell

The 3.7in HAA gun fired a fixed round, with the propellant contained in a brass cartridge case. The standard HE shell, weighing 28lb, was filled with amatol, TNT or RDX/TNT explosive.

1. Cap
2. Dome
3. Body
4. Large locking weight disc
5. Small locking weight disc
6. Trigger
7. Scape pinion
8. Regulator
9. Scape wheel
10. Detonator and detonator holder
11. Shutter

No.207 I R.O.F.(B).1941

No. 207 Mk I Fuze

At the beginning of the war, the standard British HAA shell was fitted with a No. 199 powder-burning fuze, but the latter was replaced with the more accurate Nos. 207 and 208 mechanical time (clockwork) fuzes — both were used on rounds fired by 3.7in. and 4.5in. HAA guns in 1940–41. The No. 207 Mk I fuze seen here had a maximum running time of 43 seconds. According to the manual that accompanied the No. 207 Mk I, 'The fuze relies on a clockwork mechanism consisting of a train of wheels driven by a spring or by centrifugal weights and controlled by an escapement. At the end of the time as set, the mechanism releases a lever which allows a striker to be driven onto a detonator to fire the shell's explosive magazine'.

from the Royal Navy. Although this number slowly increased as locally manufactured weapons were delivered, in early 1940, the Royal Navy, as the Senior Service, requested the return of 300 Bofors guns, reducing AA Command's stocks to just 15 per cent of its operational requirement. This shortfall was not rectified during the Battle of Britain, with just 368 produced between July and September 1940.

Firing a 2lb HE round, the Bofors' rate of fire was 120 rounds per minute, with an effective ceiling of 6,000ft.

Lewis 0.303in.

Mention should be made of the Lewis 0.303in. machine gun, not because of its effectiveness, but because it was the most numerous LAA gun in service. Designed in the United States in 1911 by Col Isaac N. Lewis, the gun was mass produced in Britain by Birmingham Small Arms and proved a reliable weapon during World War I. At the outbreak of World War II, thousands of the obsolete Lewis guns (both aircraft and infantry weapons) were quickly converted and made ready for AA use. Lewis guns were widely provided for the local AA defence of airfield, searchlight and HAA

The crew of this 3in. 20cwt HAA gun have manned their weapon and prepare to elevate the barrel prior to firing. The traverse and elevation gunners needed to keep close tabs on their 'follow the pointer' dials located just under the barrel. Their movements had to match the information calculated by the predictor and displayed on the dials. (Author's Collection)

The 40mm HE AA round fired by the Bofors gun was a true aircraft killer. Fighters rarely survived a single hit and twin-engined bombers like the Do 17 were vulnerable as well. A single round in a fuel tank, the cockpit area or engine often resulted in the loss of the aircraft. (Author's Collection)

positions. Mounted in single, double and quadruple configurations, the Lewis gun was fed from either 47- or 97-round drum magazines and had a rate of fire of 500–600 rounds per minute to an effective range of 880 yards.

Hispano-Suiza Mk 1 20mm

In quantitative terms, the Hispano-Suiza 20mm LAA gun was deployed in the fewest numbers, with just 40 listed in service on 21 August 1940. Superior to the 0.303in. Lewis gun in the LAA role, the Hispano-Suiza cannon fired shells that could inflict considerable damage to a low-flying aircraft. A Swiss design, the Hispano-Suiza Type 404 was license built by the British as an aircraft cannon with the designation Hispano-Suiza Mk 1 20mm. A drum-fed (60 rounds per drum) weapon, its rate of fire varied between 650 and 700 rounds per minute. The Mk 1 had a muzzle velocity of 2,750–2,900ft per second, and apart from firing HE, other rounds including ball and incendiary high explosive (HEI) were used. HE and HEI rounds had an explosive filler weighing between 0.21–0.39oz. During the July–September 1940 battles, the Mk 1 cannon suffered from a general shortage of ammunition, particularly tracer rounds. Most Mk 1s were deployed as single units, but a few were made into triple mounts to increase their firepower. Where and how many Mk 1s – all of which were assigned to fixed sites – were allocated to vital points (VPs) is not known, but most would have been found defending RAF airfields and CH/CHL sites of No. 11 Group in southeastern England during the summer of 1940.

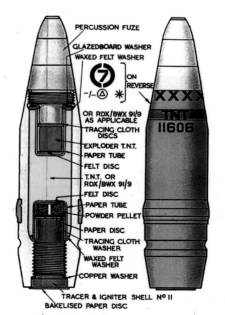

SHELL, Q.F., HIGH EXPLOSIVE, 40 M.M.

PERCUSSION FUZE
GLAZEDBOARD WASHER
WAXED FELT WASHER
OR RDX/BWX 91/9 AS APPLICABLE
TRACING CLOTH DISCS
EXPLODER T.N.T.
PAPER TUBE
FELT DISC
T.N.T. OR RDX/BWX 91/9
FELT DISC
PAPER TUBE
POWDER PELLET
PAPER DISC
TRACING CLOTH WASHER
WAXED FELT WASHER
COPPER WASHER
TRACER & IGNITER SHELL Nº 11
BAKELISED PAPER DISC

TNT 11606

✱   MONOGRAM OF FIRM OR STATION FILLING
-/-   DATE OF FILLING (MONTH & YEAR)

VICKERS-ARMSTRONGS PREDICTOR No. 1 Mk III

HAA guns were usually deployed in half-batteries of four weapons. Each set of four guns had its own Barr & Stroud No. 1 Mk IV height-finder and a Vickers-Armstrongs Predictor No. 1 Mk III. The latter was essentially the 'brains' of the system, being vital for accurate AA fire. As an electro-mechanical computer, its function was to take height and range data from the optical range finder and compute a firing solution for the guns – elevation, direction and fuze setting. All this information was electrically transferred to the guns, where the gun layers moved the weapons to match the 'follow the pointer' dials. The shortage of predictors and height-finders meant the older 3in. 20cwt HAA guns had to fire over open sights.

To increase firepower, Lewis machine guns were often grouped in twin and quadruple mounts. This twin mount, manned by RAF personnel in defence of an airfield in France in early 1940, uses Mk III aircraft guns fed by 47-round magazines. Each weapon also has a muzzle booster to increase its rate of fire. (Author's Collection)

BARR & STROUD Mk IV HEIGHT/RANGE FINDER

Once an aircraft or formation was sighted and correctly identified, the height and range had to be quickly determined so that it could be engaged by HAA guns. Manned by a crew of four, the Mk IV was a massive piece of equipment, and once the height and range had been assessed, this information was fed into the Predictor No. 1 Mk III.

GUN LAYING Mk I RADAR

Introduced early in the war, the GL I operated on frequencies in the 54 to 84 MHz range. The term gun laying, however, was a misnomer. The GL I had not been designed for the task, and was more accurately described as a 'gun assisting radar'. While it could provide accurate ranges, the azimuth indications were inaccurate and there was no elevation data. By the summer of 1940 AA Command had about 200 radars in service.

To improve the GL I's performance, the Cossor Company modified the GL I so that it gave better azimuth accuracy and provided limited elevation measuring capabilities. While accuracy improved, the data provided gave only an approximate position of an enemy aircraft, limiting the gunners to firing a box barrage in front of their target. In early 1941, the GL II radar entered service, giving gunners more accurate azimuth and elevation information.

SEARCHLIGHTS

In the summer of 1940, the most common searchlight was the 120cm SL projector type rated at 210 million candle power. At the beginning of the Blitz the 150cm 510 million candlepower searchlight became more

widely used, along with the SLC 'Elsie' radar that was fitted directly to the searchlight itself. An SLC 'Elsie' radar-equipped searchlight served as the master searchlight for a section of three smaller lights. Even when fitted with radar, and despite being able to illuminate target aircraft up to an altitude of 20,000ft, searchlights were never effective, and rarely assisted in the destruction of enemy bombers.

SOUND LOCATORS

At the beginning of the war the most modern sound locator type available was the Mk V. HAA and searchlight batteries relied on sound locators – particularly during the early months of the Blitz – to detect the approach of an incoming bomber at night or when cloud cover was present, despite pre-war testing having shown that the Mk V was wholly inadequate for the job. The latter fact meant that sound locators were rapidly being replaced by radar at the time of the Battle of Britain. The operators of sound locators used sound ranging to determine the distance between a given point and the position of a sound source by measuring the time lapse between the origin of the sound and its arrival at the listening location. The theoretical maximum detection range of the Mk V was about three-and-a-half miles. At that distance it would take 18 seconds for the noise of an approaching aircraft to reach the locator, and during that time an He 111 or Ju 88 flying at 180mph would travel four to six miles from the point at which it had first been detected. This huge lag in time meant the locator's bearing would be off by the same amount. Furthermore, a small formation of bombers would swamp the locator with noise, rendering it useless.

Prior to the introduction of radar to direct searchlights and AA guns, ground defence units had only sound locators to assist them in the detection and tracking of enemy aircraft at night. The Mk V sound locator, which was the most modern type available at the beginning of the war, was barely effective when tracking the engine noises from a single aircraft. If more than one aeroplane was present in its area, a sound locator became swamped and produced little usable information. (Tony Holmes Collection)

LUFTWAFFE BOMBERS

He 111

The He 111 was the principal medium bomber of the Luftwaffe's *Kampfgeschwadern*, and it would serve on every front on which the Germans fought during World War II. On the eve of the Battle of Britain, the He 111H had almost entirely replaced the He 111P series. The majority of the aircraft deployed during the Battle of Britain were He 111H-1s, -2s, -3s and -4s. The next variant to join the *Kampfgeschwadern* was the He 111H-5. Widely used during the Blitz, the H-5 had additional wing fuel tanks and two external bomb racks, each capable of lifting 2,205lb. The H-5 carried most of the heavy bombs and parachute mines expended during the campaign, but with the additional weight and greater drag, handling and performance were adversely affected and the aircraft required specially trained crews to deliver these heavy loads. The other specialised He 111 variant was the *X-Gerät*- and *Y-Gerät*-equipped pathfinders of KGr 100 and KG 26. These aircraft were easily recognisable, being fitted with three dorsal aerial masts that earned them the nickname *Dreimaster* (Three-master).

He 111H-2 Specification	
Type:	twin-engined monoplane bomber
Crew:	pilot, navigator, bomb aimer, ventral and dorsal gunners
Dimensions:	
Length:	53ft 9.5in. (16.40m)
Wingspan:	74ft 1.75in. (22.60m)
Height:	13ft 1.5in. (4.00m)
Weights:	
Empty:	17,760lb (8,015kg)
Max T/O:	29,762lb (13,500kg)
Performance:	
Max speed:	200mph (322km/h)
Range:	1,224 miles (1,970km)
Powerplant:	two Junkers Jumo 211A-3s
Output:	2,200hp (1,640kW)
Armament	Six or seven MG 15 7.92mm machine guns in nose, beam, dorsal, ventral and (optional) tail positions; maximum bomb load of 4,410lb (2,000kg) in bomb-bay
Production:	1,208 He 111H/P were built in 1939–40

Camouflaged in washable black distemper applied for the Blitz in the autumn of 1940, a He 111H from an unidentified unit sits at an airfield in northern France ready to be armed with two SB 1000 1,100lb *Luftminen*. Before and during the Battle of Britain/Blitz, the Luftwaffe mounted continuous mine warfare operations, with 9. *Fliegerdivision* being formed as a dedicated unit for sowing air-dropped mines in the approaches to British ports. Sea mines (high-capacity SB 1000 *Spezialbombe* or *Luftmine*) were also used against land targets during the Blitz, with the first examples probably being dropped on London on the night of 16–17 September. (Tony Holmes Collection)

Do 17

The Do 17Z was the least effective, and least numerous, of all the Luftwaffe medium bombers. Compared to the He 111 and Ju 88, it lacked the range and bomb load capability. Sometimes referred to as the *Fliegender Bleistift* ('flying pencil'), the Do 17Z was derived from a high-speed mail aeroplane/airliner and was later converted into a *Schnellbomber*. The Do 17Z's layout was unique, with two shoulder wing-mounted engines and twin-tail fin configuration. Entering service in early 1937, the Do 17 proved popular amongst its crews thanks to the aircraft's exceptional handling qualities and low-altitude performance. From the beginning of the war, the Do 17Z was assigned to low-level, short range 'battlefield interdiction' and airfield attacks. By July 1940, the Do 17Z was considered obsolescent, although it still equipped eight *Kampfgruppen* in *Luftlotte* 2. Only two *Kampfgeschwadern* were still flying the Do 17Z two months later, with a third converting to the more capable Ju 88.

Do 17Z-2 Specification	
Type:	twin-engined monoplane bomber
Crew:	pilot, navigator, bomb aimer/gunner and flight engineer/gunner
Dimensions:	
Length:	51ft 10in. (15.8m)
Wingspan:	59ft 1in. (18m)
Height:	15ft 0in. (4.56m)
Weights:	
Empty:	11,486lb (5,210kg)
Max T/O:	19,482lb (8,837kg)
Performance:	
Max speed:	255mph (410km/h)
Range:	628 miles (1,010km)
Powerplant:	two BMW-Bramo 323P Fafnirs
Output:	1,972hp (1,472kW)
Armament:	Up to eight MG 15 7.92mm machine guns in nose, rear upper cockpit, cockpit sides and ventral gondola; maximum bomb load of 2,205lb (1,000kg) in bomb-bay
Production:	887 Do 17Zs were built in 1939–40

Ju 88

The Ju 88 was the Luftwaffe's first modern purpose-built medium bomber. The RLM's 1934 specification called for a new multipurpose *Kampfzerstorer* (battle destroyer), but a year later this was cancelled in favour of a *Schellbomber* (fast bomber).

This new design could carry 1,764lb of bombs at a maximum speed of 311mph. Unfortunately, the inaccuracies of the Zeiss *Lofternrohr* 3 bombsight convinced Generaloberst Ernst Udet, the new *Generalluftzeugmeister*, to insist the new *Schellbomber* have a dive-bombing capability. The result was a much heavier and slower aircraft. Nevertheless, the Ju 88 was more versatile and faster than the He 111, had a greater range and carried a heavier bomb load. When used as a dive-bomber, it was far more accurate and

Also featuring blacked-out undersides for the *Blitz*, this Ju 88A-5 from KG 1 is fuelled at Roye/Amy in the early spring of 1941 in preparation for the coming night's mission to England. (Tony Holmes Collection)

efficient. Entering service in March 1939, the Ju 88A-1 was well liked by its crews despite initially suffering from inflight engine fires. A further redesign produced the A-4 and A-5 variants, with an increased wingspan and better handling. As production ramped up, both Do 17 and He 111 units began to convert to the Ju 88. By the end of September 1940, the aircraft equipped four complete *Kampfgeschwadern*, with five more units in the process of conversion.

Ju 88A-1 Specification	
Type:	twin-engined monoplane bomber
Crew:	pilot, navigator, bomb aimer/gunner and flight engineer/gunner
Dimensions:	
Length:	47ft 2in. (8.43m)
Wingspan:	65ft 10.50in. (20.08m)
Height:	15ft 11in. (4.85m)
Weights:	
Empty:	16,975lb (7,699kg)
Max T/O:	22,840lb (10,360kg)
Performance:	
Max speed:	292mph (470km/h)
Range:	1,696 miles (2,730km)
Powerplant:	two Junkers Jumo 211Bs
Output:	2,400hp (1,790kW)
Armament:	Five or six MG 15 7.92mm machine guns in nose, rear cockpit and ventral gondola; maximum bomb load of 4,409lb (2,000kg) in bomb-bay and underwing racks
Production:	1,885 Ju 88As were built in 1939–40

Ju 87 STUKA

At the beginning of the war, the Luftwaffe's most accurate bomber was the much-feared Ju 87B. To avoid enemy AA fire, the Luftwaffe's medium bombers were forced to drop their ordnance from between 13,000–16,000ft. At these altitudes bombing accuracy was poor, and this led directly to the Luftwaffe's obsession with dive-bombing. Capable of diving at angles of up to 80 degrees, the Stuka could deliver up to 1,500lb of ordnance with great accuracy but only at short range (the Ju 87R had a larger radius of action thanks to additional internal tankage and the fitment of external tanks). As a bombing asset, the Ju 87B was limited in its contribution during the Battle of Britain, and it was used sparingly at night during the Blitz. Although the Ju 87 units badly damaged three CH radar stations and seven airfields during the early stages of the

The Ju 87B/R Stuka dive-bomber had been used with devastating effect during the campaigns in Poland, Norway, France and the Low Countries. However, it did not fare well against RAF fighters during the Battle of Britain, and losses were high. These unarmed B-2s from 5./StG 2 are seen returning from a mission en masse. As one of the most accurate bombers in the Luftwaffe's inventory, Stukas were also the most difficult to deter with AA fire. If they were not engaged during their approach, which was made at around 15,000ft, the Ju 87s were fleeting targets once in their dives. LAA gunners had just ten to 15 seconds to track and fire upon a diving Stuka before pull-out. (Andy Saunders Collection)

campaign, loss rates were far too high. During just six days of combat (12–18 August), 41 Ju 87s were shot down by fighters and AA fire. Shortly after, the Stukas were withdrawn from the attack against targets in England.

Ju 87B-1 Specification	
Type:	single-engined monoplane dive-bomber
Crew:	pilot and rear gunner
Dimensions:	
Length:	36ft 5in. (11.10m)
Wingspan:	45ft 3.2in. (13.80m)
Height:	13ft 2in. (4.01m)
Weights:	
Empty:	5,980lb (2,713kg)
Max T/O:	9,369lb (4,250kg)
Performance:	
Max speed:	211mph (339km/h)
Range:	490 miles (788km)
Powerplant:	Junkers Jumo 211Da
Output:	1,100hp (820kW)
Armament:	Two fixed MG 17 7.92mm machine guns in wings and one MG 15 7.92mm machine gun on flexible mounting in rear cockpit; maximum bomb load of 1,102lb (500kg) on centreline and four 110lb (50kg) bombs under wings
Production:	697 Ju 87B-1s, 225 Ju 87B-2s, 105 Ju 87R-1s and seven Ju 87R-2s

Bf 109E and Bf 110D

The Bf 109E-4/B and Bf 110D-0 fighter-bombers were arguably the most successful Luftwaffe bombers during the Battle of Britain, with ErprGr 210's low-level attacks proving a problem for British defences. Compared to the much-vaunted Ju 87, which was struggling in the face of determined attacks by RAF Fighter Command, the fast-moving precision strikes by the *Jabo* unit were a welcome success for the Luftwaffe. As the first variant of Messerschmitt's outstanding single-seat fighter to be bomb-equipped, the Bf 109E-4/B was simply an E-4 equipped with the ETC 500 stores rack located on the fuselage centreline. The aircraft's Achilles' heel was its limited range and endurance – the same problems that had plagued it when given the task of escorting medium bombers during the Battle of Britain. The Bf 110D-0 was equipped with two ETC

The Luftwaffe was the first air arm to turn its fighters into effective fighter-bombers in World War II. The Bf 110D could lift 2,204lb of bombs at speeds in excess of 300mph. By comparison, the British Fairey Battle, which was designed for battlefield support, could carry 1,000lb of bombs at a speed of just 257mph. This aircraft, assigned to ErprGr 210, has two SC 500 bombs attached to the ETC 550 racks affixed to the underside of the fuselage immediately below the pilot's cockpit. (Chris Goss Collection)

550 racks, located just below the pilot's cockpit, and it could lift two SC 500 1,100lb bombs. Ironically, as the number of *Jabo* increased in late September, the Luftwaffe changed tactics and used the Bf 109 as a horizontal bomber for attacks on London.

Bf 109E-4/B Specification	
Type:	single-engined monoplane fighter-bomber
Crew:	pilot
Dimensions:	
Length:	28ft 4.5in. (8.61m)
Wingspan:	32ft 4.5in. (9.86m)
Height:	8ft 2.3in. (2.48m)
Weights:	
Empty:	4,685lb (2,125kg)
Max T/O:	5,235lb (2,374kg) with one SC 250 550lb (250kg) bomb
Performance:	
Max speed:	348mph (560km/h) at 15,000ft (4,572m)
Range:	410 miles (659km)
Powerplant:	Daimler-Benz DB 601Aa
Output:	1,175hp (864kW)
Armament:	Two fixed 20mm MG FF cannon in the wings, two fixed MG 17 machine guns forward of the cockpit and one SC 250 550lb (250kg) bomb or four SC 50 110lb (50kg) bombs on a centreline rack
Production:	211 Bf 109E-4/Bs

Bf 110D-0 Specification	
Type:	twin-engined monoplane fighter-bomber
Crew:	pilot and radio operator/gunner
Dimensions:	
Length:	39ft 8.5in. (12.09m)
Wingspan:	53ft 4.75in. (16.27m)
Height:	13ft 6.5in. (4.12m)
Weights:	
Empty:	9,920lb (4,509kg)
Max T/O:	12,120lb (5,509kg) with two SC 500 1,100lb (500kg) bombs
Performance:	
Max speed:	349mph (561km/h) at 22,960ft (6,998m)
Range:	530 miles (852km)
Powerplant:	two Daimler-Benz DB 601A-1s
Output:	2,200hp (1,618kW)
Armament:	Two fixed 20mm MG FF cannon in the lower nose, four 7.92mm MG 17 machine guns in the upper nose, one MG 15 7.92mm machine gun on flexible mounting in the rear cockpit and two SC 500 1,100lb (500kg) bombs on a centreline rack

THE STRATEGIC SITUATION

On 9 April 1940 the Germans invaded Denmark and Norway in Operations *Weserübung* (Weser Exercise) *Süd* and *Nord*, and just a month later Operation *Westfeldzug* (Western Campaign) was unleashed across the Netherlands and Belgium, then into France. Both campaigns cost AA Command dearly, robbing it of vital guns for the upcoming Battle of Britain/Blitz. Lt Gen Frederick Pile, who had been head of AA Command since October 1939, was asked to sacrifice two HAA and five LAA regiments, the latter being equipped with 72 precious 40mm Bofors guns, for the British Expeditionary Force (BEF) in France and troops fighting in Norway. All were left behind when British forces completed their final withdrawal from both countries during June 1940.

To make matters worse, the Admiralty had also requested 800 Lewis guns from AA Command stock to help defend Norwegian and Danish merchant vessels that had recently come under Royal Navy control following the occupation of Norway and Denmark.

On the morning 10 May 1940, the largest air offensive yet mounted in the history of modern warfare was unleashed against the combined might of the Dutch, Belgian and French armed forces and the BEF. More than 500 Luftwaffe bombers, and their fighter escorts, set out for targets in the Netherlands, Belgium and France. The first to be bombed were six airfields in the

Netherlands – by the end of the day, half of the 124 operational aircraft fielded by the Dutch air force had been destroyed. By 14 May, the Netherlands had little left to fight back with, and after the devastating bombing raid on Rotterdam that killed 874 civilians, the Dutch surrendered. While the German victory had been swift, the Dutch had put up an heroic defence that inflicted significant losses (including destroying or disabling 232 Ju 52/3m Luftwaffe transports) on the enemy.

For Belgium, the Luftwaffe attacks were equally decisive, with its air force losing 135 of the original 178 aircraft it had on strength on 10 May in the first 48 hours of the campaign.

Incredibly, thanks to accurate intelligence, both the Dutch and Belgian armed forces knew the hour of attack, and were able to disperse their aircraft in preparation. The British and French, however, were taken by complete surprise, and initial attacks on 47 of their airfields resulted in the loss of 60 French and six RAF aircraft.

Hitler's *Westfeldzug* moved forward at a great pace during the first 48 hours of the campaign. On 13 May, the three armoured divisions controlled by Generalmajor Heinz Guderian arrived at Sedan, in France, to begin their two-day assault across the Meuse River. Thanks to air superiority over the battlefield, the Wehrmacht erected four pontoon bridges with little interference from the Allies. The latter tried to mount daylight bombing attacks, but aircraft were met by swarms of Bf 109Es and deadly mobile Flak batteries, resulting in heavy losses and no damage being inflicted on the bridges.

Once over the Meuse on 15 May, Guderian pivoted his armoured divisions and began a rapid drive towards the Channel coast. By the 17th the Allied situation in northern France was quickly deteriorating and panic began to set in. Guderian's headlong dash had significantly reduced the number of airfields available to RAF fighter reinforcements. By 20 May the rapidly advancing Panzers threatened the RAF's remaining bases, forcing the BEF's aircraft to be withdrawn from France.

Since the start of the campaign, Allied airfields had been frequently strafed by low-flying Luftwaffe aircraft, especially Bf 109s. Even though the BEF had set up six mobile early warning radars, five of them in a widely scattered line from Boulogne to Le Cateau-Cambrésis and the sixth at Bar-le-Duc behind the Maginot Line, they had short, uneven ranges and numerous blind spots. Their performance was poor, and provided little or no early warning of incoming raids.

For the BEF and RAF personnel targeted by those attacks, the low-level strafing passes were constant and destructive. Lt Col John R. Kennedy, who was seconded to the 23rd (Northumbrian) Division from the Royal Engineers, recalled:

The Luftwaffe had been impressive throughout the BEF's time in France. The usual tactics were dive-bombing and low-level attacks, which proved very terrifying as fast fighter-bombers skimmed through the trees, and men found themselves momentarily seized by the instinct to

stand and watch. There was a great necessity for educating men to take cover at once, and to fire back at the aeroplanes as quickly as possible.

In terms of HAA fire for the BEF, the 3.7in. gun was at best unproven, as high-level attacks were few, but when it came to LAA fire, Kennedy stated that the Bofors was 'very good indeed'.

By 24 May the Allied armies were in a fighting retreat, finding themselves defending a large boot-shaped area encompassing Dunkirk, Lille and Bruges. It was here that the *Führer* ordered his Panzers to stop and form a defensive line. Hitler wanted to preserve his tanks for the final victory against the remaining divisions of the French army, believing the surrounded Allies would try to break out of the 'Dunkirk–Lille Pocket' and rejoin the French forces south of the Somme, thereby sacrificing themselves in attacks against the well dug-in Panzers and anti-tank guns. In a twist of fate, Generalfeldmarschall Hermann Göring proclaimed his Luftwaffe could easily destroy the surrounded troops at Dunkirk, and Hitler duly granted his wish.

The plan (Operation *Dynamo*) to rescue the BEF and French troops was quickly developed by the Royal Navy's Dover Command. A huge number of ships were committed, including a cruiser and 41 destroyers, along with 12 French destroyers. For the troops trapped in the pocket, AA defence was provided by the Royal Artillery's 1st, 4th, 6th and 85th HAA Regiments and 1st, 51st, 53rd and 58th LAA Regiments. The French army also had approximately 148 HAA and 45 LAA guns in the Dunkirk area. Unfortunately for the beleaguered troops, although AA weaponry was plentiful, ammunition was in short supply and was soon exhausted.

To prevent the Luftwaffe from disrupting the evacuation by sinking the ships attempting to rescue the troops off the beaches and harbour at Dunkirk, the RAF tried to provide continuous fighter cover over the area. It was a near impossible task. Outnumbered and out of range of the new CH early-warning radar system on the Kent coast, RAF Spitfires and Hurricanes had only 20 minutes' flying time over Dunkirk. Despite mounting Luftwaffe attacks, the evacuation continued, and by 31 May 126,000 Allied troops had been ferried to safety.

On 1 June Göring finally realised his plans for victory by air power alone were rapidly slipping away. Rushing back from his looting expedition in the Netherlands, he implored his commanders to finish the job. In response, the Luftwaffe mounted its largest attack on the 1st, with 160 bomber and 325 Stuka sorties being flown. Five separate raids were undertaken, and they were opposed by 270 fighter sorties. Losses on both sides were heavy, with 17 RAF fighters destroyed and the Luftwaffe losing four bombers, two Ju 87s, seven Bf 109Es and three Bf 110Cs. That day, 64,429 Allied troops were evacuated, but the price was high. Some 17 ships, including four destroyers, were sunk, resulting in Operation *Dynamo* being called off the following day and all remaining ships withdrawn from Dunkirk by 2330 hrs on 2 June.

The evacuation of the BEF and a considerable number of French troops was considered to be the Luftwaffe's first major defeat, and some historians mark it as the real beginning of the Battle of Britain. While the RAF did its best to protect the skies over Dunkirk, the Luftwaffe's inability to destroy the BEF and French defenders and prevent their escape by sea had more to do with its failure to sustain such a high tempo of operations. Over the ten days of *Dynamo*, the Luftwaffe mounted substantial raids on just three of them. Luftwaffe losses totalled 42 bombers and 36 fighters to RAF fighters and four Ju 87s and two Ju 88s to AA fire from naval vessels. It appears that no aircraft fell to land-based AA weaponry.

During *Dynamo* the Royal Navy and its French counterpart evacuated 196,649 British and 141,577 French troops to Britain. The British Army left behind 63,879 motor transports, 2,794 artillery pieces, including 120 3in., 48 3.7in. and 101 precious 40mm Bofors guns, and an untold number of 0.303in. light machine guns.

Germany's triumph in the West was astonishing. In under three months the Wehrmacht, Luftwaffe and Kriegsmarine had defeated the armed forces of Denmark, Norway, the Netherlands, Belgium, France and Britain's BEF. Germany seemed unstoppable, but for Hitler the *Westfeldzug* was a failure. His intent had been to knock both France and Britain out of the war so that he could be free to attack what he considered to be his real enemy, the Soviet Union. Now the *Führer* had to deal with the possibility of an amphibious invasion of the British Isles. It was an operation both the Wehrmacht and Kriegsmarine had not fully contemplated and were wholly unprepared for.

Disabled BEF 3in. guns litter the promenade at Bray-Dunes near Dunkirk following the end of Operation *Dynamo*. AA weapons such as these in and around Dunkirk quickly ran out of ammunition, leaving the air defence of the port and evacuation to RAF Fighter Command. In addition to the thousands of lost vehicles, artillery pieces and tanks, the British Army left behind 76,000 tons of ammunition and 165,000 tons of petrol in France. (Andy Saunders Collection)

For the British, *Dynamo* had been an unexpected triumph, although Churchill (who had only been made prime minister on 10 May 1940) was quick to recognise what had just happened. While the number of troops evacuated was impressive, it was a humiliating defeat. In many respects, if the 'the miracle of Dunkirk' had not occurred, the profound sense of defeat, shock and fear of imminent invasion could have swayed British public opinion and shifted the political landscape. The calls to acquiesce to Hitler's demands may have grown stronger and left the government with little choice. Indeed, there were some politicians and members of the Royal Family who thought to fight on was pointless.

The Allied defeat on the continent had been catastrophic, although the Germans had suffered as well. The Battle for France and the Low Countries had cost the Luftwaffe 1,092 aircrew. Despite these losses, it still remained arguably the best all-round and technically advanced air force in the world in 1940, with well-trained aircrew and a mix of proven medium bombers, dive-bombers and fighter-bombers, escorted by the outstanding Bf 109E.

Flush with victory, the Luftwaffe was about to face the most sophisticated and effective integrated air defence network then in existence. While Hurricane and Spitfire squadrons were the network's largest and most glamorous component, they were backed up by AA Command's HAA and LAA guns, barrage balloons and searchlights. Short of weapons, well-trained crews and supporting equipment, AA Command would be put to the test for the first time in World War II.

THE COMBATANTS

AA COMMAND

In October 1939, AA Command came under the operational control of RAF Fighter Command. The men who manned the guns came from Territorial Army (TA) units, and they were backed up by RAF personnel who manned LAA guns (Lewis 0.303in. machine guns and some Hispano-Suiza Mk 1 20mm) at airfields across Britain. Home Guard troops also served as gunners for a small number of Lewis and Vickers LAA weapons defending less vital targets.

In 1935, as Britain began to upgrade its AA defences, the need for more troops to operate such weapons was obvious. This led to the decision to train a number of TA infantry regiments to operate AA weaponry. Despite the formation of the 1st AA Division on 15 December 1935, recruiting for TA AA brigades remained slow. In the spring of 1938, the War Office decided the time had come to add additional AA camps to the already existing ones at Watchet, Manobier, Burrow Head, Weybourne and the first LAA camp at Stiffkey. Six HAA camps were considered necessary at this stage, with three or four more LAA camps to be ready by the spring of 1939.

46

In 1938, growing public concern about the state of Britain's air defences led to the formation of the AA Corps, which took direct charge of the AA Divisions (whose number would be increased from two to five). On 15 July 1938, Maj Gen Alan Brooke was promoted to lieutenant general and assumed command of the new AA Corps.

In the first 18 months of the war, AA Command expanded rapidly, almost tripling from 106,690 men on strength in September 1939 to more than 300,000 in May 1941. But there were problems. In the first months of the conflict, many of the men assigned to AA Command were barely worth having. The first conscripts to arrive under the Militia Act of 1939 were the weakest recruits from the rapidly expanding British Army intake. One potential gunner in four was unfit for service in any army. For the volunteer TAs already in service, this influx into their pre-war regiments represented a 'plague of dimwits'.

Manpower deficiencies led to a reduction in the number of searchlight units and, later, to the introduction of mixed units and the use of Home Guard troops to man AA equipment. Training at the outset was woefully inadequate, and when radar gun laying was first introduced many young scientists had to work and live near the HAA batteries in order to give gunnery officers technical assistance and help with the training of crews.

The manpower problem plagued AA Command throughout the war. As Luftwaffe attacks increased, a new list of Vulnerable Points (VPs) was drawn up, which called for the creation of another 200 LAA troops for their defence in October 1939 alone. Just as one gap was filled, new ones appeared.

To meet the anticipated threat of air attack, the number of AA units grew rapidly from 1938 to 1940. Initially, several infantry units were hastily converted into the AA role, and by September 1938 five new divisions had been formed. On 1 April 1939, AA Corps was upgraded to a full Command. When ordered to mobilise on 28 August 1939, AA Command was short of men and equipment – although on paper it was comprised of seven divisions. Each of the latter consisted of a mix of gun brigades and searchlight battalions. On 5 June 1940, the 1st AA Division had under its command 45 4.5in., 39 3.7in. and 26 3in. HAA guns and 19 40mm Bofors and approximately 185 Lewis machine guns in the LAA role. Added to this were 240 120cm SL projector type searchlights.

AA Command's order of battle on 3 September 1939 was as follows:

1st AA Division – Metropolitan area of London (HQ Uxbridge)
2nd AA Division – north East Anglia, East Midlands, Humber (HQ Hucknall)
3rd AA Division – Solway Firth, Scotland, Northern Ireland (HQ Edinburgh)
4th AA Division – northwest England, West Midlands, North Wales (HQ Chester)
5th AA Division – South Wales, southwest and southern England (HQ Reading)

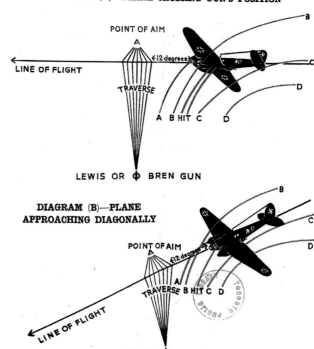

OBSERVATION OF TRACERS

Diagrams showing outline of enemy Long-Range Bomber (viz. Heinkel He, IIIK Mk. Va.), used to attack shipping in the North Sea.

DIAGRAM (A)—PLANE CROSSING GUN'S POSITION

POINT OF AIM
LINE OF FLIGHT
TRAVERSE
A B HIT C D
LEWIS OR BREN GUN

DIAGRAM (B)—PLANE APPROACHING DIAGONALLY

POINT OF AIM
TRAVERSE B HIT C D
LINE OF FLIGHT
LEWIS OR BREN GUN

The iron sights on the Lewis machine gun were of little use when trying to target a fast-moving aircraft. To improve the gunner's aim, soldiers were taught to use tracer fire. Such rounds had a pyrotechnic charge located at the base of the projectile that ignited during firing and could be easily seen. This training drawing clearly shows what represents a hit and a near miss when aiming with tracer fire. (Author's Collection)

6th AA Division – southeast England and southern East Anglia (HQ Uxbridge)
7th AA Division – northeast England (HQ Newcastle upon Tyne)

In November 1940, five new divisions were created as follows:

8th AA Division – southwest coast (HQ Bristol)
9th AA Division – South Wales (HQ Cardiff)
10th AA Division – Yorkshire and Humber Estuary (HQ York)
11th AA Division – west and central Midlands (HQ Birmingham)
12th AA Division – southwestern Scotland (HQ Glasgow)

In addition, to ease the supervision of this organisation, three AA Corps were created as follows:

I AA Corps covering the south (1st, 5th, 6th, 8th and 9th AA Divisions), corresponding with RAF Fighter Command's Nos. 10 and 11 Groups.
II AA Corps covering the Midlands (2nd, 4th, 10th and 11th Divisions), corresponding with RAF Fighter Command's Nos. 9 and 12 Groups.
III AA Corps covering the North (3rd, 7th and 12th AA Divisions), corresponding with RAF Fighter Command's Nos. 13 and 14 Groups.

For the men who manned the guns, especially those assigned to HAA and searchlight batteries, life was a mix of boredom, tedium and isolation, interjected with periods of intense and exhausting action. For those not at already established permanent sites (mostly defending ports and large cities), they often found themselves assigned to weapons/searchlights in a farmer's field, miles from even the smallest village. These positions were totally unprepared, which meant many crews had to dig and construct their own gun positions, living quarters and cooking and washing

A range finder crew (at left) and gunners training in 1940. During the Battle of Britain, AA training schools like this one were stripped of vital equipment that resulted in just five 3.7in. mobile guns and one 3in. HAA gun being available on 24 July 1940. The result was new recruits assigned to a battery had to receive on the job training, which adversely affected AA Command's overall performance and effectiveness in 1940–41. (Author's Collection)

facilities. Living under canvas was not uncommon, making life even more miserable. For LAA gunners assigned to an RAF airfield, life was much more comfortable, with access to good accommodation, a mess hall and, most likely, a pub close by.

For HAA gun crews who experienced repeated location shifts, life was even harder. *Roof over Britain*, an official account of AA Command published in 1943 by the Ministry of Information, recorded the operations of a battery assigned to the London area from the Humber defences in 1940:

> Twenty-five hours later, the battery was on its new site – a site almost completely unprepared. Ground, clogged with bricks, mortar and stone, had to be levelled. Guns had to be laid down, instruments connected and supplies of ammunition arranged. A 3-ton R.A.S.C. [Royal Army Service Corps] lorry was pressed into use as a men's canteen and another as a sergeant's mess. By 7:30 p.m. all essential work had been done and the guns were ready.
>
> At 8:15 p.m. the alarm was given. The battery opened up with a barrage which had to be worked out on the spot, as ready communication with central control was not available. At 6 a.m. the order 'Stand Easy!' was given, to the relief of four gun teams of dead-beat men. But it was only 'Stand Easy!' as far as action was concerned. There was work to be done in boiling out, servicing and polishing the guns. It was 9:30 a.m. before the men went to sleep, in tents, with the bare ground as their bed. Half-an-hour later came the first of many daylight alarms. For eight days the procedure was the same. On the ninth day relief came, in the shape of troops who had done no more than the basic military training. Only two hours were available in which to instruct them in their duties.

By mid-October 1940 there was evidence of faltering morale among the HAA troops in London. Lt Gen Frederick Pile recognised that the problem was caused partly by repeated shifts of position among the gun crews. The result was officers seldom had time

A 40mm Bofors gun is manhandled into position during a training exercise. AA Command gunners undertook physically demanding work that required a good level of fitness and stamina. A Bofors gun crew comprised six men – No. 1, NCO gun commander; No. 2, layer for bearing; No. 3, layer for elevation; No. 4 breach loader; and two 'ammunition numbers' to pass four-round clips to the breach loader. (Andy Saunders Collection)

ATS personnel operate a kinetheodolite (used to record on film the accuracy of AA shells) at the Royal Artillery AA training school at Manorbier, on the Pembrokeshire coast. In the background are two 3.7in. guns and a single 4.5in gun, as well as a pilotless DH 82B Queen Bee radio-controlled target aircraft. (Author's Collection)

to prepare their sites fully, and they lost track of spares and supplies. For the gun crews, the squalor of their accommodation did not help, nor the lack of sleep. According to Sgt John Burge of the 163rd HAA Battery/55th HAA Regiment, defending the Thames Estuary:

> During the Battle of Britain sleep was always on a cat nap basis. We stayed with the guns, we ate with the guns, and if there was a lull in the fighting we slept with the guns.

To give the HAA gunners their due, the Blitz put them under enormous strain. The difficulties they faced were not of their making, and few were within their power to resolve. Personnel shortages also continued to be a problem. In December 1940, AA Command was short 1,114 officers and 17,965 other ranks. It was a problem that Lt Gen Pile would finally vigorously tackle in the spring of 1941.

In addition to their air defence role, AA gunners and searchlight crews also had a role in ground defence. For those at airfields, their first job was to engage enemy aircraft overhead. Luftwaffe bombers were the primary target, although in the summer of 1940 AA Command believed that Ju 52/3m transports carrying paratroopers might also appear at some stage. This meant gunners also had to be prepared to engage any airborne troops who had gained a foothold on the airfield.

Generally, the invasion threat prompted a mass programme to prepare each AA and searchlight site as a defended strongpoint. To that end, in June 1940 Bofors crews were issued with anti-tank ammunition and ordered to lower their parapets so that they could engage tanks and ground forces. HAA batteries would also play an important part both as field artillery and in the anti-tank role.

LUFTWAFFE AIRCREW

When the existence of the Luftwaffe was announced in March 1935, senior officers disagreed in respect to how the new air force would function. One school promoted the idea of 'total war' in which a nation's industrial capacity, along with its workers and their homes, were legitimate targets. Others saw air power in tactical terms, there to support the Wehrmacht directly. And then there were those like senior staff officer Oberstleutnant Helmuth Wilberg, who believed the Luftwaffe could be both a strategic and tactical air force.

Even before the first He 111s and Ju 88s had flown, a requirement for a Ural bomber was issued as early as 1932. This called for a four-engined bomber with sufficient range to strike targets in the USSR or British assets like the Royal Navy base at Scapa Flow. Two prototypes in the form of the Dornier Do 19 and Junkers Ju 89

SIR FREDERICK A. PILE

In the final six months before the outbreak of war between Britain and Germany there were increasingly anxious attempts to bring AA defences into readiness for the feared 'knock-out blow'. On 1 April 1939, AA Command came into being, and in October of that same year Lt Gen Frederick Pile was made its General Office Commanding-in-Chief.

Lt Gen Sir Frederick A. Pile, known to his many friends as 'Tim', was a late arrival on the AA scene. He was an unusual officer. The son of a Protestant Nationalist baronet, he was an Irish aristocrat, and his early upbringing was, as he described it, spent in a political atmosphere that leaned 'decidedly to the Left'. Compared to his army contemporaries, Pile had no public school background. Indeed, due to his erratic tutoring, he had virtually no formal education.

Getting into the British Army proved difficult for Pile. The stringent academic standards of the Royal Military Academy at Woolwich proved daunting, and he failed in his first attempt. After intense application at a North London crammer, he did gain admittance, scraping by at the bottom of his class. Joining the military at just 18 in 1902, Pile's early academic struggles in the British Army probably reinforced the humility and generosity for which he was subsequently well known. Two year later, he passed out of Woolwich with a credible record and was assigned as an artillery officer to regiments in South Africa and then India, before finally seeing action in France during World War I. In his book *Ack–Ack*, Pile wrote little of his experiences in the Great War and nothing of his Mentions in Dispatches and the Military Cross and Distinguished Service Order awarded to him.

In the 1920s and early 1930s Pile spent his time in tanks, having transferred to the Royal Tank Corps in 1923. By 1927 he had risen in the ranks to command the Experimental Mechanised force, whose manoeuvres ironically prefigured the *Blitzkrieg* tactics later perfected by the Wehrmacht. In 1928, Pile became Assistant Director for Mechanisation at the War Office. During his four-year stint there, he worked on new light and medium tanks and mechanised artillery for the British Army. In 1932, in an odd turn of events, Pile was posted to command the Canal Infantry Brigade in Egypt. From there he was sent home to take charge of the TA-manned 1st AA Division in the autumn of 1937.

His division's primary responsibility was the defence of London, and at the time Pile was thrust into the world of AA gunnery at a pivotal point in its inter-war history. The responsibilities he inherited were onerous – defend Britain's capital, and do it without the best tools for the job. In 1938 AA Command had just 252 HAA guns and 969 searchlights available.

Pile proved to be an able and bold commander. In September 1940, at the beginning of the Blitz, London's AA guns were achieving very little in the way of downing enemy

Lt Gen Sir Frederick A. Pile (Andy Saunders Collection)

bombers. In a risky and audacious decision, he gathered his entire London staff and told them that their batteries were to cease trying to aim rounds accurately and simply focus on barrage fire. Pile informed his men to worry less about shooting down aircraft and simply put up a lot of bursts to worry the enemy and hearten the civil population'. It did both. On the night of 11–12 September, 35 London gun sites fired a total of 13,221 HAA shells into the sky over the city. This barrage fire forced Luftwaffe aircraft to fly higher, affecting the accuracy of their bombing. The following day, the Home Intelligence Division found a renewed spirit in London. 'Morale has jumped to a new level of confidence and cheerfulness since the tremendous AA barrage'.

At the end of the war AA Command was credited with downing 833 enemy aircraft over Britain. Much of its success was directly due to Lt Gen Sir Frederick Pile – he was knighted on 1 January 1945. Less than three weeks before victory in Europe on 15 April 1945, Pile retired from AA Command. He was the longest-serving senior Allied commander in a single role. Churchill had an abiding faith in Pile, who, by the end of the war, was one of the most effective leaders in the British Army. In 1945, Pile's final duty was to write a dispatch. This was followed by his book *Ack–Ack*, published by Harrap at the end of 1949.

Pile was 61 when he left the British Army. His next career was as director-general of housing in the Ministry of Works. After a brief stay, he became director of the Cementation Company in 1945, rising to chairman in 1961. Pile would go on to live a long life, before passing away on 14 November 1976, two months after his 92nd birthday. AA Command was finally disbanded on 10 March 1955, with point air defence becoming exclusively an RAF responsibility.

flew at the end of 1936. Both were equipped with chronically underpowered engines that lacked superchargers, resulting in poor performance.

The arrival of the He 111 in April 1937 led Generalleutnant Albert Kesselring, the Luftwaffe's Chief of Staff, to cancel both bombers. His reasoning was straightforward. A larger bomber took up twice the resources – fuel, engines and aluminium. He concluded that the shorter-ranged medium bomber could perform both the strategic and tactical roles. This meant twice as many bombers could be produced. Generalfeldmarschall Hermann Göring, the Luftwaffe's commander-in-chief, was in full agreement, being quoted as saying, 'The *Führer* will never ask me how big our bombers are, but how many we have'. A four-engined bomber also meant doubling the number of aircrew that required training.

When war broke out the Luftwaffe was organised around individual *Luftflotten*. Each had its own complement of bomber, fighter and reconnaissance units. They were very flexible and designed to support army units in the field. The stunning victories in 1939–40 proved the concept, but on the eve of the Battle of Britain, when it came time to formulate a concise strategic plan, inherent weaknesses in the *Luftflotten* structure began to show.

In 1940, the Luftwaffe was arguably the best all-round air force in the world, but by the end of June of that year it was already in decline. Production of replacement aircraft was not keeping pace with combat and non-operational losses. On 4 May 1940, on the eve of the western offensive, the *Kampfgeschwadern* had a total strength of 1,758 bombers, of which 1,180 were serviceable. By the eve of the Blitz on 7 September, that number had shrunk to 1,436, with just 879 serviceable. But even with these diminished numbers, bomber aircrew were well-trained and equipped with world-leading navigation equipment.

In terms of doctrine and tactics, the Luftwaffe was at a disadvantage. The Germans had never envisaged a strategic campaign against Britain, and due to poor intelligence, they underestimated the power and efficiency of the world's first integrated air defence system, which included fighters, HAA and LAA guns, searchlights and barrage balloons.

On the eve of the Battle of Britain, the Luftwaffe had some of the best-trained bomber crews in the world. There was already a cadre of airmen with real war experience following their participation in the Spanish Civil War, while many more had fought in the campaigns in Poland, Scandinavia, the Low Countries and France. Pre-war training focused on quality over quantity, but as attrition rates began to rise, instruction was shortened to make up the losses.

At the beginning of 1935, prospective Luftwaffe aircrew attended the following courses at either a *Flieger-Ersatzabteilung* (FEA – Air Training Battalion) or *Flieger-Ausbildungsregiment* (FAR – Air

Many Luftwaffe pilot cadets who failed to make the grade, but had shown enough aptitude, were sent to observer, wireless operator, flight engineer or air gunner schools, respectively. A typical He 111 crew usually consisted of a pilot, observer, radio operator and flight engineer. Some aircraft carried a fifth man who was a dedicated air gunner, but the radio operator and flight engineer also doubled-up in this role. Here, a He 111 ventral gunner readies his 7.92mm MG 15 machine gun for action. Luftwaffe bomber crews had little or no armour protection, making them vulnerable to AA fire. (Author's Collection)

Training Regiment) for six to 12 months of basic training. Aircrew then undertook a two-month course at a *Fluganwärterkompanie* (Air Cadet Company), followed by *Fliegerführerschulen* (Pilot Schools) A/B at an FEA/FAR airfield for 100–150 hours of flying training. Bomber crews were then posted to a *Fliegerschule* (Air Training School) C for a further 60 hours of flying. *Blindflugschule* (Instrument Training School) added an additional 50–60 flying hours. Finally, three months were spent at a *Waffenschule* (Operational Training School) or other specialist schools. Observers (*Beobachter*) were trained to fly to C standard, then spent up to 12 months at *Aufklärungsfliegerschulen* (Reconnaissance Flying Schools) learning the specifics of their tasking, including instrument flying training.

A Do 17Z of I./KG 2 practises a low-level airfield attack. Due to its good handling characteristics, the Dornier bomber was used exclusively in the low-level role during the Polish campaign in September 1939 and in Operation *Westfeldzug* in May 1940. Similar attempts at such missions in the Battle of Britain proved costly for Do 17Z units. (Chris Goss Collection)

After would-be bomber pilots had logged 150 flying hours, they received ground training in advanced aeronautical subjects and flew obsolete operational types such as early-model He 111s, Ju 52/3ms and Do 17Es. After a further 50–60 hours, a pilot could fly his aircraft by day or night with reasonable proficiency. At this point they would team up with their full crews and commence combined training. Flying the latest operational types, crews usually remained together. After accumulating at least 250 flying hours, both the pilot and his crew were sent to *Ergaenzungseinheiten* (operational training units) attached to frontline *Geschwader* or *Gruppen*. There, they learned the tactical and formation methods subsequently used on combat operations.

Like their RAF counterparts, Luftwaffe bomber crews flew in formations that were designed to provide the best mutual and concentrated fire support from their gunners. RAF intelligence noted that 'bombers usually approach their objectives in sub-formations in line astern, each sub-formation consisting of three, five or seven aircraft in 'Vic' formation, so disposed that they are mutually supporting'. To reduce exposure to accurate AA fire, the Germans relied on height and speed during the bomb run. In both cases, for protection against fighter attacks and AA fire, it was essential to maintain a tight formation at the best speed and height above the target.

One of the key contributions AA fire made in 1940 was the breaking up of formations by damaging bombers – when the latter fell out of formation they were sitting ducks to fighter attack. Gefreiter Willi Gailer of Do 17Z-equipped 6./KG 3 recalled his last combat mission over England on 28 August 1940, when his unit targeted Rochford airfield, in Essex:

I remember we were ordered to attack an air base – I do not know where exactly – and while flying over England in formation, we were hit by anti-aircraft fire and our aircraft lost speed and fell back. After a while we were far behind our *Staffel* and were attacked

Aircrew from an unidentified Ju 88 *Kampfgeschwader* conduct an open-air mission briefing in front of a suitably camouflaged bomber at an airfield in northern France during the early weeks of the Blitz in October 1940. (Getty)

by two Spitfires. Being the *Bordfunker* (Radio Operator), I had to handle the upper rear machine guns, so I tried to keep the attacking fighters away from us, as did my comrade Flieger Anton Brückmann, who fired the bottom rear gun. I am sure that one of the fighters was hit by our gunfire because he did not carry out further attacks against us. The other Spitfire continued to attack us and I became seriously wounded, with the result that I was unable to shoot back any more.

I remember the pilot, Leutnant Peter Krug, tried to escape by flying the aeroplane at low-level straight back to our base at Antwerp, but he had no chance. As far as I still remember, we finally ditched in the Channel and the aeroplane sank immediately. We were then picked up by English fishermen, taken back to England and I was sent to hospital.

This example clearly shows that the combination of AA damage and fighter attack was almost always fatal. Morale and crew efficiency also suffered. Constant operations and having to watch the death and wounding of fellow crewman by AA fire took its toll. As casualties mounted, Generalfeldmarschall Hermann Göring issued an order that crews were to include only one officer per bomber.

In August alone, Luftwaffe medium bomber crews suffered 91 pilots killed and 104 missing to both fighters and AA fire. By September the percentage of operational crews and established aircraft strength had dropped to an unacceptable level. For the crews who faced AA fire and fighters on a daily basis in 1940, the psychological and mental toll was heavy. Personnel began to refer to the English Channel as the 'dirty ditch', and a number of them developed what they called *Kanalkrankheit* ('Channel sickness').

HUGO OTTO SPERRLE

At the beginning of the Battle of Britain, Generalfeldmarschall Hugo Sperrle was the most experienced air campaigner in the Luftwaffe, and the only high-ranking field commander with any understanding of air power and its proper application. Known for his coarse wit and gross table manners, Hugo Otto Sperrle was the son of a Württemberg brewer. Born in 1885, he joined the army at the age of 18 and became a Leutnant in the *Infanterie-Regiment* 'GroBherzog Friedrich von Baden' Nr.126, subsequently training as a balloon observer. From there Sperrle transferred to the expanding *Luftstreitkräfte* (Army Air Service).

As aircraft were introduced, Sperrle continued to serve as an observer with *Feldfliegerabteilung* (FFA – Field Flying Detachment) 4, later commanding FFA 42. Earning his wings, he was badly injured in a crash in February 1916. Following a long recovery, Sperrle commanded an observer school and was later promoted to *Kommandeur der Flieger* (Aviation Commander) for *7. Armee*, covering Alsace at the southern end of the German front.

After the war, he initially served in the *Freikorps* and was then part of the air staff for *Wehrkreis* (Military District) V in Stuttgart, commanding a handful of small government mail/ army courier units. The latter were equipped with wartime AEG J.II and LVG C.VI ground attack/observation aircraft and mainly flew between Berlin and Weimar. Starting in the mid-1920s, and in breach of the Treaty of Versailles, Sperrle commanded the observation school at the clandestine training centre at Lipetsk, in the USSR. In 1927 he replaced Oberstleutnant Helmuth Wilberg as head of the air staff at the secret Waffenamt and Truppenamt (Weapons and Troop Offices).

During the Nazis' rapid expansion of the Luftwaffe between 1933–35, Sperrle was considered the *Reichsluftwaffe*'s expert on air power, and its battlefield application. He was soon chosen to lead the new Luftwaffe's first tactical command, *Fliegerdivision* (Flying Division) 1, which was established in Berlin in April 1934. With the outbreak of the Spanish Civil War in 1936, Hitler decided to support General Francisco Franco's Nationalists with air power. Sperrle was chosen as the first commander of the *Legion Condor*, an independent air force of 120 aircraft, 5,000 men, 1,500 vehicles and five Flak batteries. Initially flying 'first generation' Heinkel He 51 fighters and Ju 52/3m bombers, the *Legion Condor* was quickly outclassed by the Soviet fighters and bombers supporting Republican forces. Sperrle soon began to receive the latest He 111s, Bf 109s and Ju 87s, which quickly redressed the balance in the air over Spain.

Returning to Germany in October 1937, Sperrle was promoted to *General der Flieger*. Six months later, he was given command of *Luftwaffengruppenkommando* 3, which later became *Luftflotte* 3, based in Munich. In 1938 his command participated in the annexation of Austria, followed by the subjugation of Czechoslovakia in 1939. During the invasion of Poland in September 1939, *Luftflotte* 3 was held in reserve in the event of any military response from France – its strength was reduced to just two bomber wings and eight fighter groups at this time. Shortly thereafter, and in preparation for Hitler's *Westfeldzug*, *Luftflotte* 3 was expanded to three *Fliegkorps* with seven bomber and seven fighter wings (588 bombers and 509 fighters), plus one Stuka wing with 103 Ju 87s. In July 1940 Sperrle was promoted to Generalfeldmarschall. With his headquarters in Paris, Sperrle's *Luftflotte* 3 occupied bases in the French capital and as far west as Brest and Vannes.

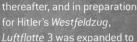

Generalfeldmarschall Hugo Sperrle (Tony Holmes Collection)

Sperrle was one of the few Luftwaffe commanders who understood how air power should be applied. On 3 September 1940, when Göring and Hitler announced their intention to bomb London as a prime target, Sperrle disagreed. He believed the offensive against airfields, sector stations and other RAF ground installations should continue. He seriously doubted Luftwaffe intelligence that claimed just 100 British fighters remained as of 17 August after the RAF had lost 1,115 aircraft up to that point. He estimated the RAF Fighter Command had 1,000 fighters. Despite Sperrle disagreeing with Göring and Hitler, it was his bombers that delivered the first blow on London when, on the night of 6–7 September, 25 aircraft dropped 26.9 tons of HE and 50 incendiary canisters on the docks in East London.

Sperrle was still in command of *Luftflotte* 3 when the Allies launched Operation *Overlord* on 6 June 1944, although it was a mere shadow of its former self. Sperrle had just 600 aircraft of all types available, with only 152 fighters serviceable. In two weeks of combat *Luftflotte* 3 lost 75 per cent of its aircraft. Sperrle was dismissed from his post on 24 August 1944. He was eventually captured by the Allies in May 1945 and charged with war crimes, but was acquitted not once, but twice – firstly, at the Nuremberg High Command Trials in 1948, and later at a second hearing before a court in Munich in 1949, which concluded that he had never been a member of the Nazi Party. Sperrle died in Munich on 2 April 1953.

COMBAT

The Luftwaffe started its offensive against Britain in early June 1940, with probing nocturnal attacks on airfields, ports and industrial areas. For example, on the night of 19–20 June, 70 He 111s of KG 4 attacked targets in East Anglia. This was the largest raid mounted on Britain to date, and it cost the Luftwaffe five aircraft to nightfighters. It could be said that the German air assault on Britain (*Lufschlacht am England*) commenced with this attack. For the month of June, Luftwaffe bombers targeted 13 airfields, 16 industrial plants and 14 port areas, mostly at night.

The defenders claimed 16 aircraft destroyed, but only eight were confirmed. Just one aircraft was downed by AA fire, with the rest being shared between Blenheim IFs (four) and Hurricanes and Spitfires (three). While these early results for RAF Fighter Command's makeshift nightfighters were encouraging, the Luftwaffe's shift in tactics (flying higher and using evasive manoeuvres) all but nullified this early success.

The next phase of the campaign began on 2 July, when *Kanalkampf* targeted shipping in the English Channel and the ports of Southampton, Portsmouth, Portland and Dover. Protecting the latter was a combined HAA defence of 24 4.5in. and 85 3.7in. guns, as well as AA weaponry on naval vessels in port. Almost daily, three *Fleigerkorps*, along with low-level attacks by *ErprGr* 210, attacked convoys carrying coal from Wales to London. A total of 25 small steamers and four destroyers were lost, and in late July the Royal Navy was forced to withdraw its destroyer flotilla north of the Thames Estuary.

This He 111H-8 of 4./KG 27 crash-landed on a hillside in West Lulworth, Dorset, on 22 May 1941 after touching the ground in poor weather during an armed shipping reconnaissance mission. The bomber's Ballonabweiser (anti-balloon fender) aroused sufficient interest for the aircraft to be recovered and transported to the Royal Aircraft Establishment at Farnborough, in Hampshire, for further examination. (Andy Saunders Collection)

At the end of July, AA Command gunners claimed 26 victories during the course of the month, half of which were downed by the batteries protecting Dover. While more enemy aircraft were destroyed by fighters than by AA fire, the gun defences proved their deterrent value. Incoming formations were broken up and AA bursts helped signal the bombers' positions to patrolling Hurricane and Spitfire pilots. As the battle developed Luftwaffe bomber formations adopted more aggressive evasive manoeuvres. This led to formations more readily splitting up, resulting in single bombers flying widely divergent courses that made them easy prey for RAF fighter pilots.

Aside from the threat posed by AA batteries and Spitfires and Hurricanes, barrage balloons also proved effective when German bombers encountered them directly. Indeed, aircraft were almost always destroyed or severely damaged when they ran into a barrage balloon cable, for survival after such an impact was highly improbable unless the bomber was fitted with dedicated fenders – relatively few Luftwaffe aircraft had them at the time. However, one crew operating over Britain had a remarkable escape after 'landing' on top of a barrage balloon, rather than striking its cable.

On the evening of 22 July 1940, four Ju 88s of 7./KG 30 set out to drop magnetic mines into Plymouth Sound, the aircraft being led by Hauptmann Hajo Hermann. The operation culminated in a low-level and low-speed delivery of the mines in a heavily defended area. For Hermann and his crew, it would be an unforgettable mission. Approaching over the northeastern outskirts of Plymouth and heading southeast at around 15,000ft, Hermann throttled back, extended his dive brakes and trimmed the aircraft nose-up to achieve an almost flat, quiet, 45-degree descent to the release point. With the breakwater release point in sight, and searchlights stabbing the sky successfully seeking the Ju 88 out, the aircraft had dropped to around 6,000ft in bright moonlight when, suddenly, a grey bulbous mass loomed directly in Hermann's path – a barrage balloon!

With no opportunity to take evasive action, at slow speed in a semi-stalled flying attitude and with the controls unresponsive, the Ju 88 literally wallowed onto the top of the balloon rather than flying into it. What happened next was described by Hermann as 'like trying to fly a grand piano that had been thrown from a high-rise apartment!' After seconds, the bomber fell off the balloon and the crew still found searchlights shining at them. Only now they were shining from above – they were tumbling earthwards, but upside down.

With the realisation he was still alive, Hermann shouted *'Aus!'* to his crew, ordering them out of what seemed to be a stricken aircraft. A wall of cold air slammed into the cockpit as the canopy was released, and Hermann selected full throttle and closed the dive brakes. Almost immediately, and just as the crew were about to abandon the Ju 88, control was regained right above the breakwater. Releasing his mines, a shaken Hermann roared off at full throttle, chased by ground fire. Behind him, the flapping and deflating balloon descended over the city. It had been an incredible escape. Had the Ju 88 been just a few feet lower when it met the balloon, the bomber would have impacted the cable head-on. The outcome, then, would have been rather different.

While these early operations resulted in a degree of success, they were not the Luftwaffe's primary mission. On 1 August, Göring convened a large conference at the Wehrmacht occupation HQ in the Dutch city of The Hague to finalise the plans for *Unternehmen Adler* (Operation Eagle). The Luftwaffe's primary mission was to destroy the RAF, both in the air and on the ground. This also included attacks on radar and communication sites, aircraft production plants and supply infrastructure and the destruction of Royal Navy vessels in port and at sea along England's southern coast. More directly, the Luftwaffe had to gain total air superiority over southern England to protect the Wehrmacht's amphibious invasion.

The first targets would be Britain's CH radar sites and selected airfields in southern England. The opening attack – called *Adlertag* (Eagle Day) began on 12 August. The missions flown during the course of the month were a mix of high-level medium bomber, low-level fighter-bomber and dive-bombing attacks.

Prior to the onslaught commencing, AA Command had identified 217 VPs that were protected by 3,538 LAA guns of seven types and a small number of 3in. HAA guns. Just 227 40mm Bofors were sited, which meant no fewer than 86 per cent of the LAA weaponry comprised rifle-calibre Lewis machine guns. Many of the Bofors lacked predictors, with gunners having to rely on 'forward area sights' – essentially visual shooting.

Fighter airfields were the best defended, especially those in No. 11 Group, whose area covered much of southeast England. The most heavily protected airfield was Manston, on the eastern tip of Kent. It bristled with four 40mm Bofors, six Lewis guns and eight 3in. HAA guns. Each radar station in No. 11 Group also had three 40mm Bofors. In contrast, some 141 VPs were defended solely by Lewis guns. In terms of HAA weaponry for airfield defence, no 3.7in. guns were assigned, leaving just 35 3in. HAA guns to defend the airfields of No. 11 Group.

On 12 August the first raids on the coastal elements of the air defence system began. One of the most effective attacks was mounted by 66 Ju 88As of KG 51 and III./KG 55 against Portsmouth and the Ventnor radar station on the Isle of Wight.

Hauptmann Hajo Hermann, seen here as a highly decorated Oberst later in the war, was fortunate to survive a close encounter with a barrage balloon whilst attempting to drop magnetic mines from a Ju 88 into Plymouth Sound during the evening of 22 July 1940. Serving with 7./KG 30 at the time, Hermann flew more than 320 missions during the early campaigns of World War II. (Tony Holmes Collection)

OPPOSITE

In southern England in 1940–41, the airfields and CH radar stations of the RAF's Nos. 10 and 11 Groups, along with the ports of Southampton, Portsmouth and Dover, were the most heavily defended sites in the entire country.

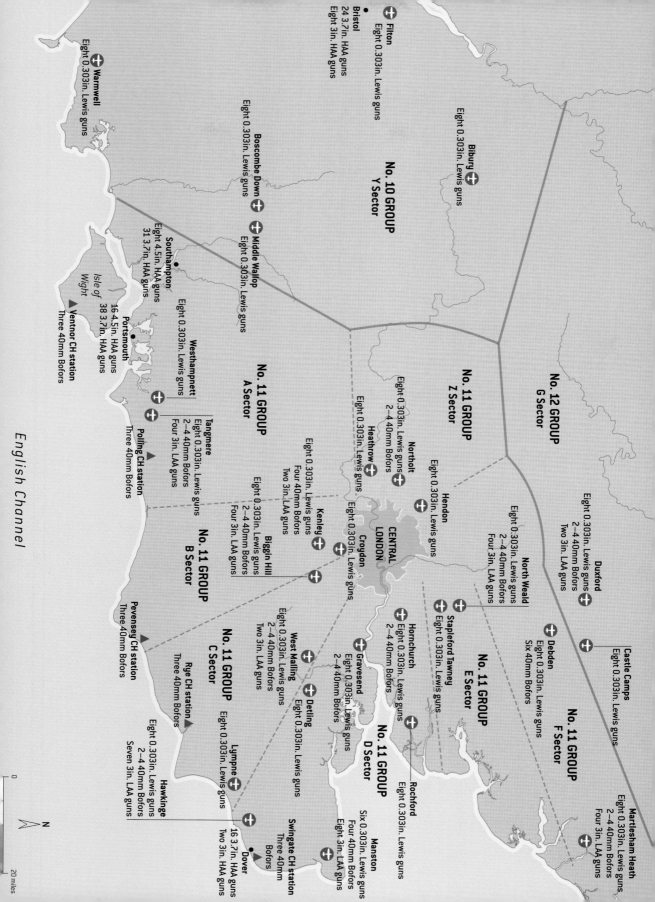

The Luftwaffe opened *Adlerangriff* (Eagle Attack) on 12 August with a series of raids on four CH radar sites along the southeast coast. It used a mixed force of Bf 109/Bf 110 *Jabos* for low-level raids and Ju 88s bombing from high altitude. Aside from aerial attacks on the vitally important radar stations, the Germans also used long-range artillery sited on the French coast to try and neutralise the CH stations. In this photograph (taken by the Germans from the Calais coast), the CH radar installation at Swingate, near Dover, is under attack from the air. Note the barrage balloons deployed to defend the site from dive-bombers and *Jabos*. (Andy Saunders Collection)

For Oberleutnant Werner Lüderitz of *Stab/KG 51*, this would be his last mission:

On the morning of 12 August, the *Kommodore*, Oberst Dr. Hans Fisser, received by telephone from the Chief of Luftwaffe 3 in Paris, Generalfeldmarschall Hugo Sperrle, the order to carry out an attack by all serviceable aircraft against the radar station at Ventnor and the harbour facilities, yards, fuel dumps and ships at Portsmouth. The secondary objective was to lure out British fighters, which would be destroyed by our escorting fighters, allowing us to establish air superiority over southern England.

The *Kommodore* decided that the attack *Geschwaderstab* would take part in the attack on the radar station. The bomb load for the attack was either two SC 1,000kg bombs or four SC 250kg bombs – my aircraft, coded 9K+AA, was loaded with two 1,000kg bombs.

We rendezvoused over Le Havre at an altitude of 5,000m and headed for England. After overflying the eastern half of the Isle of Wight, we turned eastward and split up – *Geschwaderstab* and II. *Gruppe* towards Ventnor from the north, whilst I. and III. *Gruppen* turned towards Portsmouth. We came down at a 70-degree angle in a loose formation from 4,000m, released the bombs at 1,200m and intended to climb from 800m to transit home in level flight. However, the port engine quickly lost power and stopped – during the dive, we had been targeted by a lot of Flak, and shrapnel hit the port engine and interrupted the fuel supply. We remained far behind the formation, which was climbing, and I took the necessary steps for asymmetric flight. We found ourselves alone over the Isle of Wight at about 1,000m, flying south and still trying to gain height.

Shortly after crossing the coast, we were attacked by three Hurricanes. As a result of evasive manoeuvres, we had lost height very quickly and were, after five or six attacks, about 50m above sea level and expected to ditch. However, as we had been told that coastal waters around the United Kingdom had been mined, we turned towards land. After further attacks while we were very low, I put the aircraft down wheels up. We crashed through hedges and the aircraft burst into flames.

This day also saw daylight attacks on Kentish airfields at Hawkinge, Lympne and Manston. Although they had some of the best LAA defences in Britain, only the Manston guns claimed a victory in the form of a Bf 110.

On 13 August – *Adlertag* – the Luftwaffe targeted 13 airfields. The results achieved were somewhat less than expected, and the units involved suffered heavy losses. A total of 1,484 sorties were launched and 42 aircraft shot down, two them claimed by AA fire. Airfield and radar station attacks continued between 14–18 August. On the 15th, the satellite airfield at Lympne reeled under sustained blows from Ju 87s that put it out of action for two days. At Hawkinge, Do 17s, He 111s and more Ju 87s delivered a low-level and dive-bombing raid, with the LAA gunners claiming four damaged and one aircraft downed. This same attack also targeted nearby Hythe, Folkestone and Dover, where a fierce AA battle raged resulting in a total of 11 claims being made.

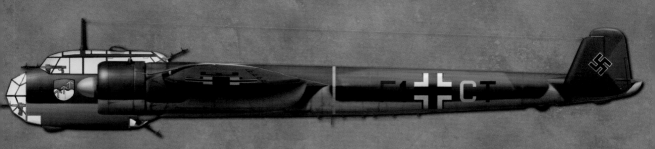

Do 17Z-3 F1+CT of 9./KG 76, Cormeilles-en-Vexin, France, 18 August 1940

Both the low- and medium-level attacks by Do 17Zs on Kenley on 18 August 1940 caused extensive damage to the Surrey airfield, although the Luftwaffe paid a heavy price. Four of the low-flying Dorniers from 9./KG 76 were shot down by AA fire and fighters and the remaining five damaged to varying degrees. F1+CT was amongst the latter, its pilot, Feldwebel Adolf Reichel, managing to coax the bomber across the Channel before crash-landing near Abbeville. Of the four-man crew (which included a war correspondent), only Unteroffizier Albert Haas was lightly wounded.

On this day the effectiveness of *EprGr* 210 and its fighter-bombers was on full display. Sixteen Bf 110s and eight Bf 109s swept in and attacked Martlesham Heath airfield in Suffolk. The LAA gunners had no warning, and the resulting damage included two hangars and the station workshops destroyed, putting the base out of action for 48 hours.

By the evening of the 15th, the Luftwaffe had completed 1,950 sorties against ten RAF airfields, with two being knocked out for two days. Losses included seven *Jabos,* 12 Bf 110s, 11 bombers and seven Ju 87s.

For AA Command , 15 August had been a good day. Pile's men claimed 30 aircraft, 11 in the defence of Dover alone. However, like RAF Fighter Command pilots, AA Command's gunners chronically overclaimed. Verifying successes was difficult, and in order to simplify the procedure new terminology was introduced in which aircraft definitely 'destroyed' were listed as Category I claims, aircraft 'probably destroyed' were classified as Category II and those 'damaged' were Category III.

On 16 August the Luftwaffe made heavy attacks on airfields in Kent and Sussex, with approximately 1,700 Luftwaffe sorties being flown, but only nine aircraft were claimed destroyed by AA guns from the 45 confirmed as shot down that day. Airfield attacks were renewed on the 18th, with Kenley, in Surrey, being hit hard in one of the most dramatic AA actions of the campaign. The airfield was initially subjected to a low-level attack by nine Do 17s of 9./KG 76, with a further 50+ Dorniers then following up with a high-level pass. Low-level attacks had proven successful during the Battle of France, with KG 76 specialising in such missions, and each aircraft from 9. *Staffel* being armed with a 20mm Oerlikon MG FF cannon in the nose for strafing.

Flying 60ft above the English Channel, the nine Do 17s were undetected by British radar. The Dorniers had not passed unnoticed, however, for the Observer Corps' Post K3 at Beachy Head, in East Sussex, spotted the bombers as they crossed the coast. It reported the raiders' strength and heading. After a 45-minute flight, the Do 17s arrived just south of Kenley. Thanks to the efficient plotting by the Observer Corps, the airfield's ground defences were ready. They met the raiders with a mixed bag of

On 18 August 1940, nine Do 17Zs of 9./ZG 76 set out to attack the RAF Fighter Command airfield at Kenley. 9. *Staffel* was a specially trained low-level bombing attack unit. Flying at just 50ft above the Channel, hoping to avoid radar detection, the bombers were spotted by an Observer Corps post near Beachy Head, on the East Sussex coast. The raiders were then tracked as they headed inland, giving Kenley's defences ample time to prepare for the impending attack. The airfield was protected by four 40mm Bofors guns, two obsolete 3in. LAA guns and eight Lewis 0.303in. machine guns. The airfield was also equipped with a line of nine untested PAC launchers.

As the Do 17s streaked across Kenley dropping their loads of 20 110lb bombs, they were met with a hail of tracer fire. The aircraft flown by Oberleutnant Rudolf Lamberty was struck by a single 40mm shell that punched a gaping hole in the fuel tank in the bomber's port wing and set the Dornier on fire. As the Do 17 staggered through the air, it was set upon by two Hurricanes from No. 111 Sqn and finished off.

It was a costly raid for 9./KG 76, with two Do 17s being shot down over the target – one fell to a combination of machine gun fire and the PAC launchers. As the seven remaining Do 17s fled the target area, they were intercepted by Hurricanes of No. 111 Sqn. None were shot down, but all were damaged. Two Do 17s were forced to ditch in the Channel, two limped back to France and crash-landed and two made uneventful landings. Only one Do 17 returned without any major damage or seriously wounded crew.

antiaircraft guns – four 40mm Bofors, two obsolete 3in. guns and eight Lewis 0.303in. machine guns. The airfield was also protected by a recently installed PAC system.

As the Do 17s swept across the field from the south, the AA guns came to life. When tracers flashed past his bomber, Unteroffizier Günther Unger pushed his aircraft down even lower. Seconds later, machine gun rounds ripped into his right engine, bringing it to a smoking stop. Struggling to hold the Dornier straight, Unger's navigator hit the bomb release button. Following the lead aircraft, flown by Oberleutnant Rudolf Lamberty, was Unteroffizier Bernard Schumacher. He watched in fascination as the bombs began to fall. 'Hell was let loose. Three hangars collapsed like matchwood. Explosion followed explosion. Flames leapt into the sky'. Gunners again quickly found their range, with rounds smashing into Schumacher's instrument panel and the fuel tank in the port wing. 'It seemed as if my aircraft was grabbed by a giant. Bits of metal and stones clattered against the fuselage; something thudded into my back armour and splinters of glass flew everywhere'. His bomber soon began to lose power.

A third Do 17 was also hit by machine gun fire, killing the pilot, Oberleutnant Hermann Magin. Navigator Oberfeldwebel Wilhelm Friedrich Illg frantically leaned over the dead pilot and grabbed the controls, saving the aircraft from crashing into the ground.

With bombs gone the Dorniers attempted to make good their escape. Hugging the ground, they now faced the line of nine PAC launchers positioned between blast pens on the northwest corner of the airfield – three Do 17s were perfectly placed to be engaged by them. Nine rockets suddenly soared vertically into the air. Surprise was complete. Feldwebel Wilhelm Raab, flying the third Do 17 in the formation, had never seen anything like it:

Suddenly, red-glowing balls rose up from the ground in front of me. Each one trailed a line of smoke about one metre thick behind it, with intervals of ten to 15 metres between each. I had experienced machine gun and Flak fire often enough, but this was something entirely new.

Raab's piloting skill and instincts took over. He immediately pulled the Do 17 up, before dropping its right wing and aiming for a gap between two adjacent smoke trails. Seconds later, a hefty tug caused his machine to yaw, but it quickly straightened out. A cable had struck his wing. Fortunately, it was close to the tip and never took hold. Speeding past the smoke trails, Raab then dropped even lower and raced for home.

The line of cables also threatened the lead Dornier. Pulling up to manoeuvre between them, Oberleutnant Lamberty's Do 17 was hit by a 40mm shell. With his fuel tank on fire, the Dornier was then attacked by two Hurricanes from No. 111 Sqn. Lamberty kept the Dornier in the air long enough for three crewmen to bail out, while he and his *Staffelkäpitan*, Hauptmann Joachim Roth, crash-landed at Leaves Green, near Biggin Hill, shortly thereafter and were taken prisoner.

The only Do 17 brought down by the PAC system that day was flown by Feldwebel Johannes Petersen. The No. 4 bomber in the attack, it crossed the airfield higher than the other aircraft and had already been set ablaze by AA fire (and possibly a Hurricane) prior to striking the hanging cables. The combined drag from two parachutes sent the bomber crashing into a cottage just outside the northern boundary of the airfield.

Although the five occupants of the dwelling survived unscathed, the bomber's five-man crew perished.

The remaining Dorniers were in a sorry state, having been chased to the coast by RAF fighters. Two ditched in the English Channel, two crash-landed in France and two made normal landings, but with wounded or dead crewmen on board. Only one Do 17 returned without major damage or a seriously wounded crewman.

Minutes after 9./KG 76 made its daring low-level raid, 27 Do 17s bombed Kenley from high altitude – the latter was supposed to have preceded the 9. *Staffel* attack, but poor weather had delayed the strike. Three of the airfield's four hangars and several other buildings were destroyed on 18 August.

The Kenley raid clearly illustrated the dangers faced by low-level raiders when the element of surprise was lost and AA defences warned in advance of an impending attack. No matter the skill or combat experience of a crew, AA fire was the great leveller.

Unteroffizier Albert Bloss, a 65-mission combat veteran of 2./KG 76, found this out:

During my tenth mission against Great Britain, I was shot down on 31 August 1940. Over Hornchurch, our Dornier was attacked by anti-aircraft fire and the right engine stopped, so we were forced to leave the bomber formation. Later on we were attacked by five Spitfires. Some moments later I was badly wounded in the crown of the head, which gave me cerebral damage and total paralysis, except in the left arm. After the crash landing, we were captured. Oberfeldwebel [Heinrich] Lang was so badly wounded in the left leg that it was later amputated in hospital.

19 August marked the start of a five-day lull in the Luftwaffe's campaign. Göring took stock and his units prepared for a major change in tactics. While RAF airfields remained primary targets, the number of bombers being sent to attack them would be reduced. Göring emphasised that 'bombers were to be used only in sufficient numbers to draw up British fighters'. Consequently, twice as many fighters were needed to both escort bombers and undertake *freie Jagd* ('free hunt') operations to support the *Kampfgeschwadern*. For gunners defending airfields, this change in tactics was a bonus. It meant that fewer bombers, which were better targets than small fighters, could be engaged with more concentrated fire.

In the last days of August, the steady Luftwaffe attacks against airfields and sector stations continued, but a new pattern of substantial night raids against urban targets also emerged. Indeed, between 24 August and 6 September, the Luftwaffe's nocturnal efforts doubled, with as many as 170 sorties being flown per night. This new tactic had an inauspicious start. On the evening of 24–25 August a wayward He 111 overshot its target and dumped bombs on the East Ham and Bethnal Green boroughs of London. Churchill ordered an immediate retaliatory RAF Bomber Command strike on

Gunners from a 4.5in. HAA battery near Portsmouth pose with shells and the tail section of a Bf 109E-4 from 2./JG 2 shortly after the fighter's demise on 26 August 1940. Its pilot, Oberleutnant Hans-Theodor Grisebach, bailed out of the aircraft and was captured. During his subsequent interrogation, Grisebach stated that his Messerschmitt had been hit by AA fire during a bomber escort mission over Portsmouth, after which his damaged fighter was then attacked by a Hurricane (almost certainly flown by Belgian Plt Off A. E. A. van den Hove d'Ertsenrijck of No. 43 Sqn) and crashed east of Blendworth, near Horndean in Hampshire, at 1625 hrs. (Andy Saunders Collection)

Berlin, with raids flown on 28–29 and 29–30 August. Outraged, Hitler quickly lifted the ban on bombing London. This phase of the battle would last until early September, when the night campaign became AA Command's primary concern.

On 7 September the Luftwaffe dramatically altered its tactics, with airfields becoming secondary targets. The new primary target was now London. On this date, the first significant daylight attack (comprised of 348 bombers escorted by 617 Bf 109s) was mounted on the British capital. Opposing the raiders, AA Command had 48 4.5in. and 32 3.7in. static guns and six mobile 3.7in. batteries. Apart from duelling with the Luftwaffe over airfields, ports and radar sites, this would be AA Command's first major battle of the war.

Stacked from 14,000ft up to 20,000ft, the Luftwaffe bomber formations rendezvoused over the Pas-de-Calais and headed towards London. At 1616 hrs the defences were alerted. Between 1640–1810 hrs, bombs – including 100 of the large new 3,968lb SC 1800 'Satan' weapons – hit Woolwich Arsenal, Surrey Commercial Docks, the oil tanks at Cliffe and Thameshaven and the Beckton gasworks, which

A lone He 111 is seen over the Upper Pool of London during the late afternoon of 7 September 1940, the aircraft participating in the first daylight attack on London. The Western Dock and a portion of St Katherine Docks can be seen in front of the bomber's port wing, while the soon to be hard hit Surrey Commercial Docks are visible behind the starboard wing. (Author's Collection)

erupted in flames. It was a reasonably clear day, and as the bombers approached, batteries all over East London brought their weapons to bear. In the first hour, 18 sites engaged – including all of those flanking the Thames down-river from the docks, which was the primary target of the attack. On this day AA gunners optimistically claimed 19 aircraft destroyed. Just four He 111s and two Ju 88s were shot down by fighters and AA batteries.

The daylight attack was followed by a night raid by a further 318 bombers, which dropped 330 tons of HE bombs and 440 incendiary canisters. This was London's first heavy night attack, and it was subsequently identified as being the official beginning of the Blitz. At 2106 hrs the guns engaged, but only 185 rounds were fired and one bomber shot down, the aircraft crashing into the Thames. This was not AA Command's best showing. Most guns were late into action, gun laying radar proved of little use and the debut of the Cossor fixed azimuth network for the GL I was a huge disappointment.

By 11 September, in four nights of raids, the Luftwaffe had mounted 761 sorties over the capital. London's guns, in turn, had destroyed a confirmed total of four bombers. It was a small number, but four more than the victories claimed by the nightfighter crews of RAF Fighter Command. In every respect, AA Command's pre-war planning for London's defence had failed, and the worst was yet to come.

BLITZ

As previously noted, 7 September 1940 saw the beginning of the Blitz, the Luftwaffe's night bombing campaign against Britain. After the heavy losses suffered on daylight raids on 11 and 15 September, and with air superiority clearly out of reach, Hitler postponed *Seelöwe*. Up to this point the attrition suffered by the Luftwaffe had been telling. To begin its new night campaign, the *Kampfgeschwadern* had approximately 800 bombers (down from 1,311), with a serviceability rate of just 52 per cent.

Even before the Blitz began in earnest, the Luftwaffe had been bombing British targets at night for quite some time. One of the largest nocturnal raids occurred on the night of 27–28 August when 180 bombers attacked Liverpool. Between 1 July and 31 August, 3,000 night sorties had been flown, with limited results. Sadly, no fewer than 1,149 civilians had been killed in these raids.

By 11 September, and after four nights of nocturnal operations against London, Pile had a crisis on his hands. His guns were proving ineffective, and public morale was beginning to slip due to discontent with AA Command's defence of the capital. New orders were quickly issued. Gunners were instructed to stop worrying about aiming and simply fire. On the night of 11–12 September, London's gunners expended 13,221 rounds of HAA. Just one raider out of the 180 bombers despatched to attack the city was shot down, but the barrage did cause incoming aircraft to fly higher and, in some cases, deterred crews from entering London's Inner Artillery Zone. The result was a critical boost in morale, but it was no way to win the battle. Shortly after, London was reinforced with an additional 199 HAA guns. While AA Command's barrage fire tactic proved positive for those on the ground, its gunners expended 260,000 shells and claimed less than 12 aircraft destroyed in return.

The Blitz was essentially an AA battle. RAF Fighter Command's nightfighter force was in its infancy, although its performance slowly improved as the battle went on. For German bomber crews, the Blitz offered almost complete immunity from British AA defences. Indeed, the worsening autumn and winter weather were Britain's best defence, causing the Luftwaffe's accident rate to rise and making target location and accuracy difficult.

For AA Command, the Blitz clearly revealed its lack of preparation and pre-war neglect. Sound locators proved completely ineffective, for they gave

The image of searchlights criss-crossing the sky remains one of the most enduring symbols of the Blitz. Without radar guidance, searchlights – these are 120cm SL projector type searchlights rated at 210 million candle power – were rarely able to locate the Luftwaffe's bombers for AA Command's HAA gun batteries. (Getty)

He 111H-3 Wk-Nr 5606 V4+FA of *Stab*/KG 1, Amiens-Glisy, France, September 1940

On 11 September a force of 96 He 111Hs from I. and II./KG 1 and I. and II./KG 26 bombed London Docks. In a running fight over the city's East End, the He 111s were intercepted by no fewer than eight RAF fighter squadrons. Ten bombers were shot down, with V4+FA being one of two He 111s from KG 1 to be hit by AA fire and then finished off by Spitfires. This aircraft had been struck in an engine by shrapnel from an exploding shell, and as its crew approached the East Sussex coast, the ailing bomber had its second engine knocked out by several intercepting Spitfires. Pilot Feldwebel Johannes Sommer made a forced landing at Broomhill Farm near Camber, and a second He 111H from 6./KG 1 came down just a mile away at around the same time.

only an imprecise indication of the position of an enemy bomber. If more than one aircraft was present in the area, the engine noise overwhelmed the locators. In theory, the locators would provide the searchlights with the approximate location of an aircraft, and once 'conned' by the searchlights, the guns would engage. This proved to be far from the case in practice.

The GL I gun laying radar was also problematic. While it could offer reasonably accurate information on the range of a target, it could not provide the elevation and azimuth details required by gunners in order to locate enemy aircraft in three-dimensional space. One solution was the invention of an 'elevation finding' (E/F) attachment for the GL I set. The E/F was simply an electronic add-on. It was, however, very sensitive, and by the second month of the Blitz many London gun sites were fully equipped despite E/F's poor performance.

For technical reasons, the GL I was sensitive to where it was placed. Flat ground was best, but that rarely existed. To overcome the problem chicken wire was used. Covering the ground under the radar receiver aerials with a mat of wire out to a radius of 80 yards produced an area of uniform electrical conductivity that removed irregularities in the aerial lobe pattern and assisted in height finding. Although chicken wire significantly improved accuracy, there were still serious limitations. For example, aiming data generated by the GL I gave only an approximate position of an enemy bomber, although this was sufficient for gunners to fire a box barrage in front of the aircraft and not just into a patch of sky.

The arrival of the GL II in early 1941 gave the gunners more accurate azimuth and elevation information, and with better serviceability and training accuracy improved.

Searchlights also proved disappointing. Clouds, moonlight and the height of an attacking bomber affected searchlight effectiveness. In 1939, the Air Fighting Development Unit conducted two months of tests and concluded that 'the modern

OPPOSITE

AA Command's designated HAA gun battery sites in the London Inner Artillery Zone (IAZ) on 14 September 1940 – less than a week into the Blitz, and the IAZ was already in the process of being transformed. By the 14th, just 14 of the 65 sites remained empty, and the number of HAA guns in the capital totalled 199.

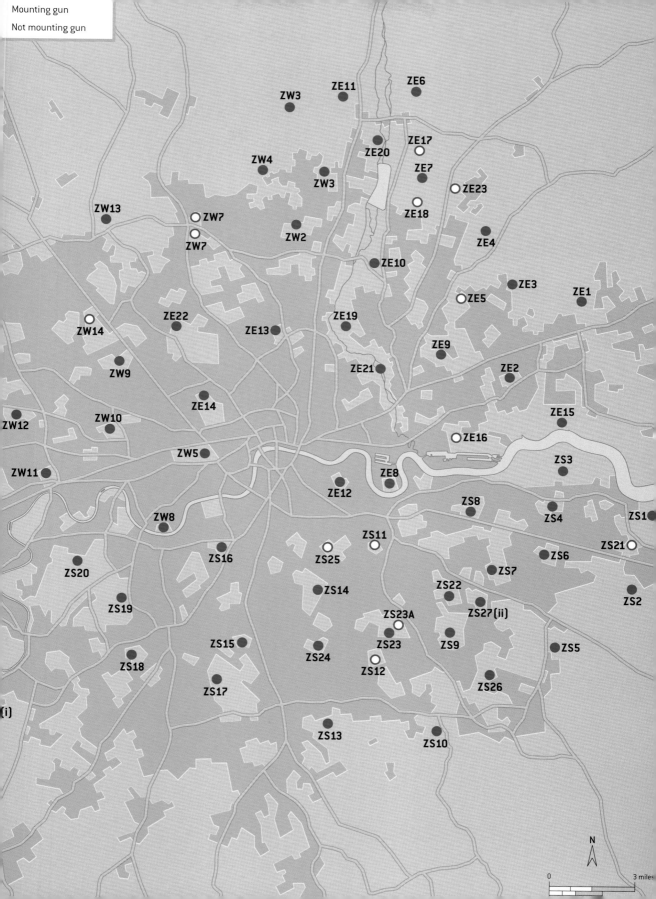

Mounting gun
Not mounting gun

ZE11
ZE6
ZW3
ZE17
ZE20
ZE7
ZW4
ZE23
ZW3
ZE18
ZW13
ZW7
ZW7
ZE4
ZW2
ZE10
ZE3
ZE1
ZE22
ZE5
ZW14
ZE19
ZE13
ZE9
ZW9
ZE21
ZE2
ZE14
ZE15
ZW12
ZW10
ZE16
ZS3
ZW5
ZW11
ZE8
ZS8
ZE12
ZS4
ZS1
ZW8
ZS11
ZS21
ZS16
ZS25
ZS7
ZS6
ZS20
ZS22
ZS2
ZS14
ZS27(ii)
ZS19
ZS23A
ZS15
ZS23
ZS9
ZS5
ZS18
ZS24
ZS12
ZS17
ZS26
(i)
ZS13
ZS10

N

0   3 miles

methods of camouflaging [matt black] night machines were such that it required about nine times as much light to effect illumination visible from the ground as was the case in the last war'. In July 1940 RAF Fighter Command received discouraging reports about the inability of searchlights to pick-up and hold high-speed targets painted matt black at heights in excess of 10,000ft.

The ZW5 half-battery of four 3.7in. guns assigned to the 84th (Middlesex, London Transport) HAA regiment fires a salvo at night from Hyde Park within the London IAZ. The sandbags indicate that this was a new temporary site established during 1940. (Andy Saunders Collection)

The crew of a night-camouflaged He 111H from an unidentified unit study a map prior to boarding their bomber at an airfield in either France or the Netherlands in March 1941. Their target for the night was almost certainly a city in southeast England. (Getty)

From the earliest night raids on Britain, the Luftwaffe's methods of attacking in darkness ranged from individual *Storangriffen* (nuisance attacks) by single aircraft to 100+ mass raids. The most frequently used technique was a continuous attack on a target over a long period of time – seven to nine hours, or as long as darkness lasted. Bombers were despatched from their airfields at intervals of about four minutes, and the aircraft flew in a stream, or *Krokodil* (crocodile), at different heights. For the AA gunners, opposing attacks of such endurance was not only exhausting, it consumed vast amounts of ammunition.

GUN CONTROL

HAA batteries and searchlights were controlled from Sector and Gun Operations Rooms. A Gun Operations Room controlled a specific gun area, giving each individual HAA site information, via direct telephone lines, about all the aircraft in its area. In addition to controlling fire against unseen targets, Operations Rooms acted as an active exchange for transmitting gunnery data from battery to battery as a raid unfolded.

Searchlights were controlled by searchlight control officers stationed in Sector Operations Rooms that were connected directly by telephone. The latter allowed a flow of information to pass from sectors to searchlight company headquarters and, finally, to searchlight sections and individual detachments.

London had borne the brunt of the Luftwaffe's wrath in September–October 1940, but in early November it widened its scope. In one of the most famous bombing raids of World War II, the city of Coventry was devastated on the evening of 14–15 November. The attack began at 1920 hrs. Guided by *X-Gerät*, the pathfinder force from KGr 100 and III./KG 26 opened the bombing. To meet the attack, Coventry was defended by just 40 HAA guns – 16 3.7in. static, 16 3.7in. mobile and eight 3in. guns. For the next ten hours, 552 bombers dropped 535 tons of bombs. AA Command's defence was fierce, with Coventry's gunners firing 6,789 rounds into the night sky during the course of 128 barrages. Just one Do 17 of KG 3 was shot down, however.

From November 1940 to May 1941, Luftwaffe bombers ranged far and wide over Britain. Targets hit – some with devastating results – included Liverpool, Birmingham, Plymouth, Clydebank and Belfast.

On 10–11 May 1941 London suffered the last major raid of the Blitz. The Luftwaffe generated 571 sorties, with its bombers inflicting the most damage of the campaign. AA gunners responded by firing 4,510 rounds. Weekly periodical *The Aeroplane* published a report on the raid that included official figures stating 33 bombers had been destroyed by both the guns and nightfighters. This was a wildly optimistic tally, for the actual claims credited to gunners in the third week of May were three-and-half shot down (one bomber was shared with a nightfighter) and three damaged.

The London attack was followed by a raid on Birmingham on the night of 16–17 May, this operation signalling the end of the Blitz. Weeks before the last bombs had been dropped on Britain, the Luftwaffe had begun moving units eastward. This was in preparation for Operation *Barbarossa* – the invasion of the USSR – on 22 June 1941. By the following month just 16 *Kampfgruppen* were left in the west, primarily tasked with anti-shipping operations.

The Gun Operations Room for the 1st AA Division situated in the lift shaft of the disused Brompton Road tube station in London. All information plotted on the RAF Group Operations Room table was copied to Brompton Road. Guns could not engage until permission had been granted by RAF Fighter Command. AA Command HQ was in direct telephone contact with all the gun sites via an open multi-phone system. Although functionally part of the British Army, AA Command came under the operational jurisdiction of RAF Fighter Command. (Andy Saunders Collection)

The wreckage of Do 17Z-3 Wk-Nr 2892 of 6./KG 3, which crashed at Prestwold Hall in Burton-on-the-Wolds in Leicestershire at 2230 hrs on 14 November 1940, killing all four crew. It had been hit by AA fire, which stopped an engine, after which the bomber was caught in searchlights and then crashed. The Dornier was the only aircraft shot down from the 552 bombers that targeted Coventry in one of the most devastating raids of the Blitz. (Andy Saunders Collection)

STATISTICS AND ANALYSIS

This poor quality, but rare, photograph shows a He 111H of I./KG 1 being targeted by heavy AA fire over the Thames Estuary en route to Biggin Hill on 18 August 1940. Shell bursts can be seen in front, below and off to the right side of the aircraft. The only aircraft lost by the unit that day fell victim to a Spitfire. (Chris Goss Collection)

For AA Command the Battle of Britain/Blitz was not its finest hour. The severe lack of guns, predictors and poorly trained crews meant results, in terms of aircraft shot down, were never considered significant in the final outcome of either campaign. But without its efforts the total number of German aircraft shot down and damaged and aircrew killed and wounded would have been much lower.

For the AA gunners, Britain's integrated air defence system, while heavily damaged at times, never broke. Despite periodic disruptions of the radar chain, the system proved robust and continued to provide ample warning for the gunners. Nevertheless, LAA performance overall was weak. The vast majority of sites were armed with single or multiple 0.303in. rifle-calibre Lewis guns, which did not have the range, rate of fire or hitting power compared to the 40mm Bofors. Add to this the poor training among the LAA crews and the results were understandable.

The rate of production of AA guns throughout the two campaigns was also painfully slow, and the demands of Britain's other colonial possessions meant many weapons went overseas. As a result, 25 airfields in Britain were equipped exclusively with obsolete 3in. HAA guns, minus predictors and range finders. This represented a token defence, and from 12 August to 6 September, during the critical phase of the battle, 53 major attacks were made on airfields, 32 of which were RAF Fighter Command bases. Just 15–20 German aircraft were claimed shot down by airfield LAA defences. With many of these airfields being sited close to London, the heavy guns in the Thames Estuary were able to play a part in their defence, but with limited results.

What Pile needed was a large stock of mobile 3.7in. guns that could be moved around to meet changing Luftwaffe operations. What he had instead was an all-too-static layout with all remaining 3.7in. and 4.5in. guns assigned to cities, ports and industrial targets.

Between January–April 1941, AA Command's stock of guns rose by just 110 (to 1,552), but in that same period 42 HAA guns went to the Middle East, 52 were sent to ports in the colonies, 16 to India and Burma and 16 to foreign customers. Incredibly, the 126 HAA weapons diverted represented a larger quota than assigned to domestic home defences. One of the reasons for the stingy allocations to AA Command was the expected arrival of UP rocket launchers. The LAA situation was no better. Between January–April 1941, just 88 40mm Bofors were added.

AA Command's most significant contribution was the decrease in Luftwaffe bombing accuracy. During daylight, HAA fire did prove effective against tight bomber formations. When accurate fire engaged the lead aircraft it often provoked evasive manoeuvres. Even without the presence of AA guns, Luftwaffe formations bombed from between 13,000–18,000ft to minimise their exposure to AA fire. There were several occasions when no AA fire was encountered and targets were, nevertheless, missed completely. Pile often pointed to the deterrent effect of AA fire, claiming that 48 per cent of bombers turned away from their targets. This was a subjective and overly optimistic number. What his critics wanted to see was wreckage on the ground, and there was very little of that.

AA fire also broke up formations, providing fighters with an easy kill. On many occasions, fighters were guided to their targets by initially spotting bursts of AA fire. The latter also damaged hundreds of bombers that subsequently needed to be repaired. This meant serviceability rates fell, and when one factors in the number of German aircrew killed or severely wounded by AA fire, combat efficiency was adversely affected. Due to a lack of effective airfield-level maintenance/repair facilities in France and the Low Countries in 1940–41, seriously damaged aircraft had to be shipped back to Germany by road/rail, or were cannibalised to keep other aircraft operational. It

The number of Luftwaffe bombers that managed to limp home despite having suffered serious AA damage during the Battle of Britain/Blitz will never be known. This He 111P of 2./KG 55 was one of them, its crew being lucky to make it back to the *Kampfgruppe*'s airfield at Dreux, in northern France, with the bomber's starboard tailplane and elevator in such a sorry state. The shrapnel holes peppering the tailfin indicate that a HAA shell exploded in very close proximity to the unusually camouflaged Heinkel during a Blitz mission in the autumn of 1940. (Tony Holmes Collection)

was not a formula for victory. Consequently, by 7 September 1940, only 52 per cent of Luftwaffe bombers remained operational.

During the Blitz, AA fire was far less effective in terms of deterring bombing accuracy. The forced switch to barrage fire meant a huge consumption of ammunition. In the month of September alone, 260,000 rounds were fired for little result. AA Command's success rate fluctuated during the campaign. In February 1941, 2,963 rounds were required to down a single bomber, and in March that number rose to 5,870. In April there was some improvement, with 3,165 shells per aircraft, but in May the number rose again to 4,610.

Even though AA fire was sometimes frightening, it was more of a distraction for Luftwaffe crews. Bombing at night presented its own set of problems when it came to accuracy. Target location, except when attacking London and eastern ports, remained difficult. Weather was the biggest limiting factor, followed by poor target marking. The lightweight incendiaries used by KGr 100 for the latter were often blown off course, causing scattered target marking. The Luftwaffe was also unable to take full advantage of its advanced beam navigation systems, as crews feared, incorrectly, that RAF nightfighters were using the emitters to home onto bombers.

Accuracy was also affected by Starfish decoy fires, which diverted five per cent of assigned raids. Decoy fires were lit 51 times between March–May 1941, with their best success occurring on 17 April when the Portsmouth decoy fire attracted 170 high explosive bombs and 32 parachute mines.

During the Blitz campaign, AA Command's effectiveness gradually improved. As Luftwaffe attacks shifted from London, AA batteries were carefully redistributed, making them more effective. The poor performance of the GL I radar, and its large blind spot, was overcome. At angles of more than 45 degrees, the GL I could not track aircraft that passed directly overhead. Beginning in January 1941, this problem was addressed by passing gun control back to Gun Operations Rooms. This allowed information from multiple GL I sets to be correlated and used to compute a firing solution that was then passed to the batteries. Searchlight effectiveness also increased with the introduction of SLC 'Elsie' radar. Initially fielded in limited numbers, SLC sets were mounted directly to 150cm 'master' searchlights with a maximum range of eight miles. But even with these improvements, the number of aircraft being shot down did not increase until May 1941.

German losses during the Battle of Britain – 10 July to 31 October, as

Attrition amongst the Luftwaffe's medium bomber crews was very high during the Battle of Britain, although survival rates improved with the switch to nocturnal missions under the cover of darkness during the Blitz. One of the most successful crews during this period was led by Leutnant Werner Baumbach (second from left) of I./KG 30, who saw action in Norway and the Battle of France, prior to flying missions over Britain. Arguably the most famous Ju 88 pilot of them all, Baumbach received numerous decorations for his success and ended the war as *General der Kampfflieger*. (Tony Holmes Collection)

officially recognised by the Air Ministry – amounted to 818 bombers (including Ju 87s) and 915 fighters to both RAF fighters and AA fire. The Luftwaffe also suffered a staggering 6,047 aircrew killed, wounded, missing or captured during the daylight phases of the campaign. These numbers confirm that AA gunners were killing and wounding a good number of Luftwaffe aircrew for no losses of their own. This gave AA Command a real advantage in the battle of attrition in 1940. By mid-September the Luftwaffe had lost a significant number of its experienced combat crews – on the 14th of that month, only 59 per cent of crews assigned to *Kampfgeschwadern* were deemed to be operationally ready.

The figure for the exact number of German aircraft downed by AA fire during the Battle of Britain/Blitz varies in published documents. In 1943, the Ministry of Information published *Roof Over Britain – the official story of the AA defences, 1939–42*. This bit of propaganda stated that AA Command was responsible for 444.5 aircraft shot down in 1940. Colin Dobinson's *AA Command – Britain's Anti-Aircraft Defences of the Second World War*, published in 2002, lists 578 aircraft claimed shot down from September 1939 through to May 1941. Considering the number of guns available and the state of AA defences during this period, both totals are overly inflated.

After the war Lt Gen Sir Frederick Pile wrote an article for *The London Gazette* titled 'The Anti-Aircraft Defence of the United Kingdom from 28 July 1940 to 15 April 1945'. In it, he noted:

> From 10 July 1940, the day which most authorities have accepted as the opening day of the battle, until 30 September 1940, the guns of Anti-Aircraft Command destroyed by day 296 enemy aircraft and damaged or probably destroyed a further 74.

After combing through the *RAF Narrative, Air Defence of Great Britain Volume II – The Battle of Britain*, published by the Air Ministry's Air Historical Branch in 1949, a more plausible but still overinflated number of 130 aircraft probably destroyed by AA fire emerges. What will never be known is the total number of Luftwaffe bombers forced to ditch in the Channel or crash-land in France due to AA damage. It must be remembered that overclaiming by fighter pilots and AA gunners was rampant. As an example, between 8–18 August 1940, RAF Fighter Command claimed 508 German aircraft shot down, with AA Command being credited with a further 88. Just 104 crashed aircraft were actually found.

During the night Blitz the Luftwaffe lost 518 bombers to all causes, of which AA Command claimed 98.5 destroyed from June 1940 through to May 1941. This is probably the most accurate figure of the two campaigns, being published in the Air Historical Branch's *The Air Defence of Great Britain Volume III – Night Air Defence, June 1940–December 1941*. AA balloons were credited with just 4.5 aircraft destroyed. How many bombers were damaged by balloon cables remains unknown, although it would have been significantly more than the 4.5 aircraft brought down.

If AA Command had had a full complement of guns and men in July 1940, its performance during the Battle of Britain and the Blitz would have been very different. German losses overall would have been higher, and with the Luftwaffe's slow rate of crew and aircraft replacement, it would most certainly have resulted in two shorter and less destructive campaigns.

AFTERMATH

When Hitler launched Operation *Fall Gelb* on 10 May 1940, his strategic aim was to eliminate Britain and France from the war so that he could turn his attention to his true enemy, the Soviet Union. The stunning victories over the Low Countries and France and the elimination of the BEF were truly remarkable, and it appeared as if it was only a matter of time before Britain surrendered. But campaigns are not won until the last battle has been fought, and the Battle of Britain in particular shattered the *Führer's* plan.

The Luftwaffe's failure to win the Britain of Britain was one of the turning points of World War II. Moving forward, from June 1941 the Third Reich was forced to fight on three fronts. Following Italy's entry into the conflict in June 1940, the Germans now had to commit troops and aircraft to the Mediterranean and North Africa. As the maritime campaign in the Atlantic increased in size, it drew more and more resources as both U-boat construction and crew training ramped up. The expectation of defeating the Soviet Union in quick order and then returning to deal with Britain never materialised. With the USSR and, from December 1941, the United States in the war, the economic and military pressure eventually exerted on Germany proved unbeatable. For the Allies, victory was not certain, but the plans set in place for the destruction of Hitler's Third Reich were.

The Luftwaffe's failure to prevail during the war's first strategic bombing campaign was finally confirmed by its performance in the Blitz. AA Command's contribution during 1940–41, while small, was significant. Without the guns, the number of Luftwaffe bombers shot down or damaged and aircrew killed or wounded would have been much smaller. So significant were the losses suffered by *Kampfgeschwadern* during the day and night campaigns that by 21 June 1941, the Luftwaffe had, in total, only 1,511 bombers available for Operation *Barbarossa*, compared with 1,711 on 10 May 1940.

The weeks that followed the last Luftwaffe night raids in May 1941 were a period of change for AA Command. Expansion remained slow while Lt Gen Sir Frederick Pile and his staff undertook a rigorous analysis of their tactics during both campaigns. New thinking and some material effects regarding deployments and procedures were incorporated, but one of the greatest changes was social, not tactical.

A shortage of manpower, which had always been an issue in the past, was addressed when the first mixed battery of men and women (from the Auxiliary Territorial Service (ATS)) became operational on 21 August 1941 in Richmond Park, in southwest London. The ATS was the women's branch of the British Army, and Pile's plan was to have 220,000 female volunteers in service by the end of 1942. This total was never realised, with Pile's complement never exceeding 74,000.

Although designated as 'mixed' batteries, women usually outnumbered men – a typical mixed battery of 388 personnel included 299 women. ATS personnel manned the radar, predictors, range finders and telephone exchanges,

ATS personnel pose in front of their Vickers-Armstrongs Predictor No. 1 Mk III. Soon after the introduction of women into AA Command during the early summer of 1941, and due to the continuing manpower shortage, the first all-female searchlight unit was formed in mid-1942. Post-war, Lt Gen Sir Frederick Pile wrote, 'the girls lived like men, fought their fights like men, and alas some of them died like men'. (Author's Collection)

and they also acted as spotters. At the time, although few were prepared to admit as much, the number of female recruits joining AA Command was, on average, higher than their male counterparts. By the end of 1944, there were more women serving in AA Command than men.

Ironically, as AA Command grew bigger, the Luftwaffe continued to bomb Britain but on a much smaller scale. *Jabo* 'nip and tuck' raids expanded during 1941–42, ending in late 1943. Individual and small groups of Bf 109 and Fw 190 *Jabos* bombed targets along Britain's southern coast for little or no military gain. Both RAF Fighter Command and AA Command had great difficulty in preventing these fast, low-level attacks. From March 1942 to June 1943, AA guns were credited with 28 *Jabos* shot down.

In January 1944, Luftwaffe medium bombers and examples of its first strategic bomber, the Heinkel He 177, returned to Britain. In a campaign codenamed Operation *Steinbock*, a force of 500 bombers was assembled to begin a new bombing offensive against London and other British cities. Between January and April nine raids were mounted against the capital. During the first three months of what was

A Bf 109E-4/B of JG 54 is loaded with a SC 250 550lb bomb. By the end of 1940, the scale and importance of raids on southern England by Bf 109E *Jabos* like this aircraft had diminished to virtually nothing. The high loss rate suffered by medium bomber units during the daylight raids in the Battle of Britain and the subsequent switch to night bombing left the *Jabos* all but redundant. Nevertheless, Bf 109 and, later, Fw 190 fighter-bombers would continue their nuisance raids throughout 1941–43. (Author's Collection)

dubbed the 'baby Blitz', 300 bombers were lost by the Luftwaffe, with AA Command claiming 49.5 victories. *Steinbock* was a complete failure due to inexperienced crews scattering their bombs over large areas when opposed by robust defences.

AA Command's last great, and most significant, battle occurred a week after D-Day (6 June 1944) when London become the target for the world's first cruise missile attack. The pilotless V1, powered by a pulse jet engine that propelled the flying bomb at speeds of up 400mph, had a range of 160 miles and carried a one-ton warhead. On 13 June the first V1s were launched from bases along the French coast. In an all-weather 24-hour campaign, an average of 153 V1s were fired per day.

To meet the new threat, AA Command was well equipped and ready. Compared to the AA Command of 1940, the gunners of 1944 had three new technical advantages. The first was the new American SCR-584 gun laying radar, which could lock-on and track targets. The second was the No. 10 Predictor, which made full use of target information from the SCR-584. Thirdly, AA shells were fitted with VT (proximity) fuses – essentially, a miniaturised radar in the nose of an AA shell that detonated the round as it passed close to an aircraft.

By July 1944, AA Command had 412 HAA and 1,156 LAA guns deployed in the defence of London. From 13 June to 1 September, 9,017 V1s were launched against Britain. Although roughly a third of them crashed on take-off, AA guns destroyed 1,459. Barrage balloons downed 231 and RAF fighters were credited with the destruction of 1,771. Nevertheless, approximately 2,450 V1s hit London.

For Lt Gen Pile, his command's efforts to defeat the flying bomb threat proved highly educational:

More was learnt about the potentialities of anti-aircraft work in 80 days than had been learned in the previous 30 years.

When the conflict in Europe ended on 7 May 1945, AA Command was the only home-based branch of the British Army to have seen continuous action throughout World War II.

FURTHER READING

AIR HISTORICAL BRANCH

The Air Defence of Great Britain Volume II – The Battle of Britain, July–October 1940
The Air Defence of Great Britain, Vol III – Night Air Defence, June 1940–December 1941
The Royal Air Force and Airfield Air Defence Since 1933

BOOKS

The Battle of Britain – RAF Narrative (Air Historical Branch, circa 1949)
Bungay, S., *The Most Dangerous Enemy* (Aurum Press, 2000)
Collier, Basil, *The Defence of the United Kingdom* (HMSO, 1957)
Dildy, Douglas C., *Osprey Air Campaign 1 – Battle of Britain 1940* (Osprey Publishing, 2018)
Dildy, Douglas C. and Crickmore, Paul F., *To Defeat the Few – The Luftwaffe's Campaign to Destroy RAF Fighter Command* (Osprey Publishing, 2020)
Dobinson, Colin, *AA Command – Britain's Anti-Aircraft Defences of the Second World War* (Methuen, 2002)
Goss, Chris, *Luftwaffe Fighters and Bombers – The Battle of Britain* (Stackpole Books, 2011)
Goss, Chris, *Osprey Combat Aircraft 129 – Dornier Do 17 Units of World War 2* (Osprey Publishing, 2019)
Goss, Chris, *Luftwaffe Fighter-Bombers over Britain* (Crécy Publishing Limited, 2003)
Hale, Julian, *Osprey Air Campaign 38 – The Blitz 1940–41* (Osprey Publishing, 2023)
Hogg, Ian V., *Anti-Aircraft – A History of Air Defence* (MacDonald and Jane's 1978)
Knight, Doug, *The 3.7-Inch Anti-Aircraft Gun in Canadian Service* (Service Publications, 2011)
Lowe, Malcolm V., *Osprey Combat Aircraft 129 – Bf 109 Jabo Units in the West* (Osprey Publishing, 2023)
Roof Over Britain – The official story of the AA defences, 1939–1942 (HMSO, 1943)
Murray, Williamson, *Luftwaffe – Strategy for Defeat* (Eagle Editions, 2001)
Nijboer, Donald, *Flak in World War II* (Stackpole Books, 2018)
Pile, Sir Frederick A., *Ack–Ack – Britain's defence against air attack during the Second World War* (Harrap, 1949)
Price, Alfred, *Osprey Elite 104 – Britain's Air Defences 1939–45* (Osprey Publishing, 2004)
Saunders, Andy, *Osprey Duel 68 – RAF Fighters vs Luftwaffe Bombers* (Osprey Publishing, 2020)
Weal, John, *Osprey Combat Aircraft 91 – He 111 Kampfgeschwader in the West* (Osprey Publishing, 2012)
Weal, John, *Osprey Combat Aircraft 17 – Ju 88 Kampfgeschwader on the Western Front* (Osprey Publishing, 2000)
Weal, John, *Osprey Combat Aircraft 1 – Junkers Ju 87 Stukageschwader 1937-41* (Osprey Publishing, 1997)
Wood, Derek, and Dempster, Derek, *The Narrow Margin* (Hutchinson & Co., 1961)

INDEX

Note: page locators in **bold** refer to illustrations, captions and plates.